Reorganising the Air Force for Future Operations

Reorganising the Air Force for Future Operations

Air Vice Marshal A K Tiwary, VSM (Retd)

(Established 1870)

United Service Institution of India
New Delhi

Vij Books India Pvt Ltd
New Delhi, India

Published   by

Vij Books India Pvt Ltd
(Publishers, Distributors & Importers)
2/19, Ansari Road, Darya Ganj
New Delhi - 110002
Phones: 91-11-43596460, 91-11-47340674
Fax: 91-11-47340674
e-mail : vijbooks@rediffmail.com
web: www.vijbooks.com

CONTENTS

Preface   vii

Abbreviations   ix

Explaination of Terms   xv

1. Introduction   1

2. Historical Analysis   8

3. The Modern World-Flat Architecture   24

4. The Modern Battle Field   37

5. Air Operations Centre (AOC)   49

6. Counter Surface Force Operations (CSFO)   66

7. Cyber Warfare   99

8. UAV Operations   113

9. Modernisation of Air Defence   117

10. Doctrine & Training   123

Bibliography   127

Index   133

Appendix

Cyberspace : Boundless Opportunity and Significant Vulnerabilities 109

"Life flits by Yudhishtira, and waits for neither you nor me. In life, there is no time for hesitation and too much deliberation. They serve no purpose but to divide the mind against itself. The thing is to act, swiftly, as the time demands."

Lord Krishna to Yudhishtira In Mahabharata

PREFACE

It is said that only thing constant is change. This can be restated that in contemporary times the only thing constant is EXPONENTIAL rate of change. This is most tellingly revealed by Thomas L. Friedman in his scholarly book, *"The World is Flat,"* published in 2006. To me this was an amazing revelation as I perused the book, particularly since I prided myself in keeping abreast with the latest.

This was also the period when the real time ISR was culminating in successful target engagement of fleeting, small targets as a routine cycle. This was a significant capability for air power which was being routinely exploited by Israel and USA.

The "World is Flat," meant a new horizontal interconnected structure of the global economy brought about by Digitisation, Internet and interdependent world economy- A result of MNCs' quest for higher productivity and resultant profits. A look at this flat world transforming the modern battlefield, revealed a tremendously transformed battle space. The militaries that embraced the modern technologies to exploit it for warfare, in effect, shrank the famous OODA loop of Col Boyd. This resulted in real time sensor to shooter cycle. The OODA loop which in past was typically in weeks and months was now reduced to minutes. Where were we in modernising our military? This question led me to undertake this research in a serious manner in 2010.

The scope of such a work can be too vast. I restricted myself to operational aspects of air power – something which had been my major occupation in my four decades of Air Force service. Also, having authored and researched books and host of articles earlier, I felt confident enough to undertake this mammoth task. Here too the field was too wide and some operational aspects, only a decade old. These were relatively new. The public literature on a subject of this nature is rare in most countries- USA being an exception. Therefore, the study extensively uses US experience, while attempting solutions to suit our needs. I am sanguine that Indian Air Force is well and truly on its path to transformation and the nature of information is such that ordinary citizens remain less informed. However, what I suggest is for an ideal Air Force to be as per my visualisation. This is in no way to suggest that Indian Air Force is not what it ought to be.

The book is the outcome of research alloted to me by USI under the Air Marshal Subroto Mukherjee Chair.

- Author

ABBREVIATIONS

A D	:	Air Defence
ADA	:	Aeronautical Development Agency(India)
AFNET	:	Air Force Network(India)
ALATS	:	Advanced Laser Targeting System
ALO	:	Air Liaison Officer
A O C	:	Air Operations Centre
ASOC	:	Air Support Operation Centre
ATCAMS	:	Advanced Tactical Missiles
ATO	:	Air Tasking Order
AWS	:	Arrow Weapon System
AWACS	:	Airborne Warning and Control System
AWST	:	Aviation Week & Space Technology
BAI	:	Battlefield Air Interdiction
BAS	:	Battlefield Air Strike
BAT	:	Brilliant Anti Tank
BVR	:	Beyond Visual Range
CAOC	:	Combined Air Operations Centre
CAS	:	Close Air Support or Chief of Air Staff
CEP	:	Circular Error Probability
CENTCOM	:	Central Command
C I	:	Counter Insurgency

CNA	:	Computer Network Attack
CONUS	:	Continental United States
COIN	:	Counter Insurgency
CONOPS	:	Concept Of Operation
CSFO	:	Counter Surface Force Operation
DARPA	:	Defence Advanced Research Project Agency(USA)
DCGS	:	Distributed Common Ground System
DHS	:	Department of Homeland Security
DRDO	:	Defence Research Development Agency(India)
EP	:	External Pilot
EO	:	Electro-Optic
ERP	:	Enterprise Resource Planning
FAC	:	Forward Air Controller
FEBA	:	Forward Edge of Battle Area
FLOT	:	Forward Line of Own Troops
FMV	:	Full Motion Video
FSCL	:	Fire Support Co-ordination Line
GIG	:	Global Information Grid
GPS	:	Global Positioning System
GWAPS	:	Gulf War Air Power Summary
HPM	:	High Power Microwave
IACCS	:	Integrated Air Command & Control System
IADS	:	Integrated Air Defence System
IAF	:	Indian Air Force or Israeli Air Force
ICBM	:	Inter Continental Ballistic Missile
ICV	:	Infantry Combat Vehicle

IED	:	Internal Explosive Device
INS	:	Inertial Navigation System
IR	:	Infra – Red
IP	:	Internal Pilot
ISR	:	Intelligence , Surveillance, Reconnaissance
IW	:	Information warfare. In USA- Irregular Warfare
JAAT	:	Joint Air Attack Team
JDAM	:	Joint Direct Attack Munitions
JFACC	:	Joint Force Air Component Commander
J FAC TSU	:	Joint FAC Training & Standardisation
J FCC NW	:	Joint Functional Component Command Network Warfare
JFEX	:	Joint Forces Exercise
JTAC	:	Joint Tactical Air Controller
JSOW	:	Joint Stand Off Weapon
J STARS	:	Joint Surveillance and Target Attack Radar System
KTO	:	Kuwaity Theatre of Opeartion
LGB	:	Laser Guided Bomb
MAAP	:	Master Air Attack Plan
MANPADS	:	Manually Portable Air Defence System
MNC	:	Multi National Corporation
MNF	:	Multi National Forces
MLRS	:	Multiple Launch Rocket System
MRBM	:	Medium Range Ballistic Missile
MTI	:	Moving Target Indication
NORAD	:	North American Air Defence

NWFP	:	NorthWest Frontier Province
NSA	:	National Security Agency(USA)
POW	:	Prisoner of War
RAF	:	Royal Air Force
RMA	:	Revolution in Military Affairs
ROE	:	Rules of Engagement
RPV	:	Remotely Piloted Vehicle
SAC	:	Strategic Air Command or Southern Air Command(India)
SAR	:	Synthetic Aperture Radar
SAM	:	Surface to Air Missile
SDB	:	Small Diameter Bomb
SEAD	:	Suppression of Enemy Air Defence
SOF	:	Special Operations Forces
SFW	:	Sensor Fused Weapons
SRBM	:	Short Range Ballistic Missile
TAC	:	Tactical Air Command (or) Tactical Air Centre
TACP	:	Tactical Air Control Party
TCP	:	Tactical Control Party
TNTT	:	Targeting Network Technology
UAS	:	Unmanned Aerial System
UAV	:	Unmanned Air Vehicle
UCAV	:	Unmanned Combat Air Vehicle
USCYBERCOM:		U S Cyber Command
WAC	:	Western Air Command
WCMD	:	Wind Corrected Munitions Dispenser

Explanation of Air Terms

Strategic : The term "Strategic" used in air warfare has meant different things, at different times to different persons. Apart from confusing the matters, it has also often generated unwanted heated debate between opposing schools of thought in air warfare.

Douhet's 'Strategic Bombing' referred to bombing of enemy population by fire and poisonous bombs, to destroy them, thereby causing such damage and terror that the nation buckles down and sues for peace. In such a war, Douhet felt that there was no need for armies and navies.

Strategic Bombing in USA and UK generally referred to intense bombing of enemy's industry to destroy its war waging, material capability, thus making hostile armies and navies as well as air forces, incapable of fighting. While Strategic Bombing occupied the main position for offensive warfare, they did not rule out armies & navies on the same scale as Douhet. This strategic bombing was also referred to as air interdiction. This AI did not need to be integrated with armies and navies. But often AI also meant attacking targets which had bearing on surface operations, like lines of communication, enemy logistics at source or in transit etc. Some targets contributed directly like attacks on POL refineries and stores. Some other targets contributed indirectly, for example destruction of electric plants, dams which powered the armament factories. Thus, the impact of AI could be long term or short term, depending upon a host of factors.

Battlefield Air Interdiction (BAI) meant targets in the battlefield that helped the army to fight the battles now or in future. To have effect, the army must be made to fight. The Luftwaffe mostly concentrated on

BAI- which makes sense if you are on the offensive. The initiative and pre war preparation makes air attacks in BAI highly effective and often immediate. A limited war would typically be characterized by BAI and least by strategic bombing or AI. This is an important consideration for the Indian Subcontinent.

Post World War II, 'Strategic' came to be associated with intercontinental ranges and heavy bombers. Tactical referred to fighter bomber. Today this is no more true. Today the so called strategic bombers like B52, B1, B2 with precision weapons often are employed for CAS, a typical tactical role. Whereas a small fighter like F-16 with its precise weapons have been used to strategic effect in destroying nuclear reactors at Osirik in Iraq and Syria. Closer home, the MIG- 21's attack with rockets on Governor's house in East Pakistan produced strategic effect, by convincing them to surrender immediately during the 71 War. So when using air force/air power, it is good to avoid debates, centred on misleading titles, like strategic or tactical air force. Rather one needs to specify the desired effect and how best to achieve it.

The intangible quality of air power – the psychological impact is equally devastating, except to the highly indoctrinated, battle hardened veterans. This quality must be used. It is not important that a pilot/UAV cannot see everything on surface. But an enemy soldier/terrorist seeing an aircraft/UAV overhead, invariably believes that his position has been exposed. We need to exploit this.

Close Air Support : 'Air action by fixed and rotary – wing aircraft against hostile targets, which are in close proximity to friendly forces and which requires detailed integration of each air mission with the fire and movement of these forces."

Comments : The above definition has virtually remained unchanged from World War I experience and is same for most militaries. In World War I, the maximum artillery range was only 5 Kms. The aircraft operating speeds were around 200 – 300 kmph. Manoeuvre war was basically a day light activity. So detailed integration was easier; fire and movement rates were lesser; combat identification of own troops, tanks and artillery was relatively easier. The modern battlefield and the battlefield of future has manoeuvre warfare 24 hours each day – night and bad weather; with rates of movement faster; aircraft speeds 3 to 4 times that of World War II; the range of artillery is around 40 – 50 kms, of multiple rocket launchers 75 – 100 kms, of tactical missiles in hundreds of km, the newer users of air space being the numerous helicopters, UAVs, UAS, C^2 planes, AWACS, air refuellers etc. In essence 'detailed integration of each air mission – with friendly troops in linear and non – linear battle fields' is an enormously complex task. The detailed integration planning, process, procedures between so many users, in real – time is no easy task. Then, to pass the required information to various agencies; for each operator to operate flawlessly for each mission, while still retaining maximum flexibility, seems Herculean, if not impossible, despite advances of technology. The confusion of war still demands simple solutions; solutions which degrade gracefully rather than catastrophic collapse. The cost benefit ratio, if one could be worked out, would lead to inevitable conclusion that immediate BAS in modern wars must be an exception, to deal with disasters than being a regular practice.

INTRODUCTION

" Never make the mistake of thinking that the validity of a proposition or the correctness of a doctrine depends upon the number of people who believe in it. As you grow older, the truth will come to you that in the fields of politics and economics, the soundness of an ideology is often in inverse proportion to the popular support it commands."

Nani A. Palkhiwala.

Periodic reviews and refinements are a constant part of organisations to keep it abreast with the contemporary standards. This includes examining necessary changes since last review; to apply new technology & suitable process; to discard the obsolescent equipment & process; to adjust the organisation to desired changes in concepts, doctrine training etc. A review of the Air Force in 2011, that too from outside the service after retirement, reveals many areas within the service which have seen only marginal changes. These minor changes probably were necessitated to absorb emerging technology, in order to make functioning more efficient. But most of these changes, at best, were sort of patch repair, a minor increment to existing models inherited post World War II. Absence of a full scale, intense war after 1971, helped in keeping us oblivious to fundamental changes needed in the organisation, to meet the demands of modern and future wars. Now a detached study from outside and comparison with more professional air forces, reveals our long neglected holistic reorganisation. This said, it is also true that one can not turn an organisation on its head just for the sake of reorganisation. Reorganisation must be a smooth and gradual process, barring exceptions. With this in mind, a brief review of some of the operational areas is being attempted. Needles to say, this preliminary review would require further in depth study in each area. So this brief review is only suggestive in nature, for in depth study by suitable agencies and personnel, dealing with it day in and day out.

Warfare extending in the third dimension of airspace is a recent phenomenon, barely a century old when compared to the recorded history of warfare going back to 5000 years. Use of ships to transport warriors is also quite ancient and is well recorded during Greek and Roman times. Yet it was only in the 18th and 19th century when proper integration of cannons, onboard ships along with the mechanical power of steam turbines, made the Navy's role the dominant part in the warfare equation. Nations that controlled the high seas became the Global powers. It was mainly the European nations, which dominated the oceans world wide, thereby carving out vast colonial empires to fuel their industrial revolution and called the shots in international affairs. The era of nations with 'Sea Power' overshadowed the fading continental powers like Russia, Austria and the Turks.

In the 20th century, the arrival of the aeroplane and consequent Air Forces would once again reshape the equation of warfare. It would usher in the concept of simultaneous 'Total War' for the first time. Now the devastation and destruction of fire power could be applied every where. The aeroplane would easily fly over the fielded armies and linear defences and strike at the very heart of the enemy nation. It would target industries and supply networks, the sinews of war machinery. It would attack the population itself as well as attack the armies and the Navies. All this could be done simultaneously if a nation had a sufficiently large Air Force, or alternatively it could be done sequentially or selectively.

The 1st World War, after a brief dynamic start with manoeuvre warfare had turned into a bloody stalemate along the 500 miles trenches in the middle of France. The various battles, characterised by massive artillery bombardment, the barbed wire defences, and the poisonous gas, consumed the youth of Europe in vast numbers. The 1916 battle of Somme lasted nearly five months, yet neither side advanced more than a few yards. British casualties numbered 419,654; French nearly 200,000; German 6,50,000.

Aeroplane, the latest invention to be introduced in the 1st World War, provided Commanders with a mobile high ground for reconnaissance over vast areas- quickly and far more accurately than by any other means so far. The quest for aerial intelligence soon resulted in aerial dogfights between opposing sides. The need to establish and maintain 'Command of Air' as had been the case with respective navies, in the not too distant past, became fundamental to exploit this high ground. Aerial bombing of the enemy heart land was also tried. Physically it did not produce the desired results. While the concept was sound, the existing technology was way behind to enable effective bombing. But the psychological terror produced by limited damage was far out of proportion. It would strongly influence the air doctrine towards the concept of strategic bombing in nearly all the nations. This obsession with bombing resulted in insufficient regard to other aspects of aerial warfare, mainly air defence.

The stalemate at the trenches, which produced casualties approaching a hundred thousand lives for gain of territory measuring mere hundreds of yards, forced the commanders to desperately break out of this logjam. Air Forces, in close air support (CAS) role provided the answer. It was the effective CAS of the allies (The British and the Americans) which turned the table on Germany. CAS was also one of the major contributors for German defeat in the Battle of Amiens.

Since World War I till the battle of Beqqa Valley in 1982 and more demonstrably in Iraq War of 1991, the concepts and practice of conventional air warfare remained little changed. The command and control organisations, the communication links, the weapons of destruction, the limitations of poor visibility, night time, and adverse weather remained. In spite of the various technological fixes attempted to overcome these, the limitations of air power persisted. It was the Iraq war of 1991 initially, followed in quick succession by air action over Bosnia in 1995, over Kosovo in 1999, in Afghanistan since 2001 and over Iraq since 2003 that has revolutionised aerial warfare. This has also affected the art of total war itself. While Israel had been demonstrating many evolutions and revolutions on a smaller scale, spread over time, it was the above major actions which caught everyone's

3

imagination world wide. This study attempts to highlight modern developments, some of which are at exponential rate and changing the face of technology, at the rate predicted by Moore' Law. Their impact on air war had resulted in unimaginable concepts till yesterday. Like a B2 strategic and stealth bomber doing a CAS mission 100 metres from own troops; in place of 1000 bomber raids, to destroy a target during World War II to current ability of a B-2 bomber to strike 100 targets in one mission with far higher assurance level and insignificant damage to civil population and infrastructure; the persistence of an unmanned air system likely to increase to weeks and months to loiter over hostile areas, detect targets, track targets and destroy them as and when commended by a controller, sitting half way across the world; etc. We need to fully understand these revolutionary changes and relate these developments to our environment. We need to review our command and control structures, our concepts, our manning policies etc. Unlike the past, the modern militaries are expected to fight across a wide spectrum of warfare, from counter insurgency (COIN) at one end to possible but unlikely nuclear war, at the other end. Being tremendously expensive and used seldom for intense wars due it's deterrence value, if the same military can help internal security matters as a possible dual role, while training for conventional war – nothing like it.

Our existing command and control structures for operations were mainly created for static land warfare along our borders. Though these structures and equipment have been periodically updated, the rate of change has been slow thus curtailing the optimum employment of air power. Our area of interest, however, has expanded from Suez Canal to Malacca straits and probably beyond. Defence of our Island territories, 1500 km from the mainland would need an expeditionary force, built on modern technology. Can our command and control organisation and operational doctrine adapt for this requirement? UN commitments have tended to increase for the peacekeeping role. Do our UN mission deployments employ suitable command and control structures integrating army, air force and navy? Non-lethal weapons are slowly but surely being used with increasing effect. Is our system flexible enough to incorporate the same? Modern systems and organisations are highly complex. These are manned by personnel whose ages range from late teens to 62 years at the very top. The grasp on modern gadgets and ability to use it to one's advantage is inversely proportional to the age of the average user. So, if younger members have better grasp on modern technology, does our system permit enough participation by younger age levels in designing and evolving our structures? Unlike the past where in, one major innovation brought revolutionary changes, today's complex organisations excel by capitalising on many small enhancements, suggested by multiple users. The enhancements are a result of synergistic participation. Is our command and control structure open and flexible enough to encourage innovations in a multidimensional participative relationship? This study will attempt to address all these issues. Mainly the issues are:

1. Our command and control structure for various air operations like CAS, AD, CAO etc., do not seem to have kept pace with the technological advancements. Is this a result of deliberate planning or lack of it? This requires a review.

2. The modern three dimensional battle space is far more complex than the earlier two dimensional battle fields when air operations made their debut. The earlier battlefield seldom exceeded depths beyond 5 km. Today's battle space is also time and information critical. It permeates into space. The reach of the army's tactical missiles in the conventional role, is 300 km plus. This needs an extremely complex system to function optimally. Where are we in this journey?

3. Airpower has global reach. We have Su-30s and AWACS plus air refuellers to operate our air power to the extremes of our area of interest. Do we have suitable command and control structures for the same?

4. In future, UAVs are likely to make question of persistence obsolete. We have UAVs in all three services, in reasonably large numbers. Their numbers will only increase. Do we have optimal system in place for their integrated utilisation?

5. GPS enables everyone to know his location precisely and most of

the time, enemy position also precisely. Have we leveraged this to our advantage, in support of each other?

6. GPS enabled bombs can be used 24 hours day & night and through weather precisely. Being GPS guided they are unaffected by the type of launch aircraft. Thus we see B-2 doing close air support. Have we factored this in our counter surface support operations doctrine?

7. Though artillery still remains an area weapon, more and more army munitions are progressing on the path to precision. Will we then still require air support in the same way as in the past?

8. Communication revolution has changed the face of civil world. It can / will do the same for armed forces, depending upon how fast we want to embrace the changes. Where are we in this quest?

9. Imageries from Satellite, aircraft, and UAVs combined with extremely fast processing and fusion makes surveillance and target fixation precise and real time. Can our command and control system exploit this fully?

10. Precision munitions have changed the nature of waging war from total war/ mass destruction to precise targeting with least damage to unintended. Does our training and armament procurement reflect this reality?

11. Future will provide increasing ability to destroy hundreds of targets in one sortie / mission / wave. How then should we plan missions?

12. Asymmetric wars / insurgencies are becoming more frequent and militaries inevitably get drawn into it. How do we build in this needed multitasking and multi training?

To arrive at proper solutions for the future, the study will begin with historical review. In modern warfare, the Western model led by USA has been at the forefront. Therefore, the historical review will focus with a heavy bias towards western militaries. The evolution of doctrinal thought and force employment from World War I, till the latest war, will be undertaken.

While the Indian Military has remained steadily focussed due to geographic and permanent nature of threats, this too is undergoing subtle changes. Our area of interest has expanded beyond coastal waters. The Island territories' defence & security has increased in scale. Anti Piracy off Somalia & in Malacca Straits, require a collaborative effort with India seen as a major partner. UN peacekeeping roles are tending towards peace enforcement operations. Is our old command and control structure built from the experiences of World War II to address continental threats, flexible enough for new challenges? Is it flexible enough to incorporate the new technology which has accelerated the pace of change to exponential proportion? Our military is getting far more involved in COIN operation. Non lethal weapons are becoming more effective. Is our model flexible enough to meet all the demands, without major changes? The study will attempt to address the above issues. No doubt it is a mammoth task, but the Chinese saying that a thousand mile journey starts in one small step, reinforces my faith in self and provides determination.

2

HISTORICAL ANALYSIS

"Out of the past is built the future. Look back, therefore, as far as you can, drink deep of the eternal fountains that are behind and after that, look forward, march forward and make India brighter, greater, much higher than she ever was."

Swami Vivekanand

In India, we inherited nearly all our concepts, doctrines, organisations and procedures from the British and adapted it to our environment and thinking. Since World War II, USA has been the undisputed leader in conventional warfare, whereas, Israel has been extremely adaptive and innovative in warfare dealing with numerically strong opposition as well as in low intensity war. Germany almost succeeded in the initial stages of World War II, till the very pace of its enormous success itself laid the foundation for ultimate defeat, due to overarching ambition. France, the most fortified country, post World War I, collapsed like a house of cards against the German blitzkrieg. Vietnam proved the futility of ill pursued war, even with massive resources when US fought with ill defined aims and methods. In Afghanistan, the unconventional asymmetric war methods adopted by the weaker side, led to defeat of superpowers, twice over.

We need to revisit the history in above cases, in order to better the plan for the future. We need to educate ourselves properly, before selecting successful models for our environment. Then alone should we attempt a review of our existing model for modern times. If we choose and adopt a wrong model, no matter how good and elaborate its command and control structure, it will not serve the purpose it was meant to. In modern, fast paced wars, there will be little time to learn from mistakes and reorganise

8

midway though a war, as was done repeatedly by eventual victors, during World War II, the Korean War, the Vietnam War etc. In this context, Israel has far more similarities, to demand special examination.

The historical examination will be country wise, dealing with major roles of air warfare and their ongoing evolution to modern times.

USA

The isolationist policy followed by USA kept her out of World War I till 6 April, 1917. Once USA entered World War I, its participation was by means of an expeditionary force. This force comprised of the Army and an Air component. By 1918, there were two primary roles for attack aircraft – to attack targets along the heavily defended front line and secondly to attack targets up to the depth of twenty miles and more behind the frontline[1]. The land battle was supported well by the air component.

However during the interwar years, the doctrine of strategic bombing overshadowed the other roles like air defence, and air support of the land forces. The bomber barons believed in victory through strategic bombing alone. This put to backseat, the successful lesson of World War I of integrated air support of the land battle. The disastrous result of the desert war in Tunisia, at the Battle of Kasserine Pass in 1943, reinforced the principle of centralized control of air assets and decentralized execution by air units in support of land forces. The belief in the strategic bomber, without first obtaining air superiority, led to a disastrous start to bomber campaign over Europe thereafter. Facing heavy attrition, to the tune of over 18%, the Bomber offensive had to be suspended for four months. Once the long range fighters, P 47 Thunderbolt and P-51 Mustang were integrated to establish air superiority, then the strategic bombing resumed.[2] Strategic Bombing, by itself failed to win the war. But indeed, its contribution to the weakening of German War machine, and the German morals were major factors in eventual defeat. In the support of ground battles, to defeat

---

[1] David A. Lee, "Close Support : Setting Conditions For Success in the Objective Force", Air University, Maxwell Air base, Alabama, USA, 2003. p.9.

[2] "The US Bombing Survey," 30 Sep 1945, A U Press, Alabama, USA, Oct 1997,pp.16-16.

Germany, the naval battle of Atlantic, the Island hopping Pacific campaign, role of air power was indeed crucial. This art and science of close air support, which had received little scholarly attention prior to the war, improved with each battle and campaign. At its peak, even the entire bomber effort was directed for interdiction, along the planned attack avenues. One popular example is during Operations Cobra, the breakout from Normandy.[3]

The atomic bombing of Hiroshima and Nagasaki on 6th and 9th August 1945, hastened the Japanese surrender. An estimated saving of 200,000 causalities resulted, which would have been the case in the absence of atom bombs' usage. This, in a way, also proved the ultimate strategic bombing role of Air power. Post World War II, independent USAF emerged with three major commands characterising USAF's roles and missions – the Strategic Air Command (SAC), The Tactical Air Command (TAC) for close air support and the Air Defence Command (ADC) to establish air superiority.

Post World War II, the funding constraints invariably resulted in inter service rivalry for funds and focus on primary service roles. The co-operation with other services suffered. Korean War from 1950-53 saw the introduction of helicopters on the battle field. In the 1960s, as Americans got involved in Vietnam in counter insurgency work, the scope of helicopters seemed to enlarge.

Armies have generally always planned for and fought with the allotted resources under their command. The aircraft and helicopters – to an army man -were yet another resource, like the artillery, the cavalry etc. to be placed under his command. The flexibility of air power – under centralized command and decentralized execution, over a geographical area equal to an aeroplane's radius of action was incomprehensible to the soldier. That this area of operation of the aeroplane lay over many Corp Commanders' area of operation, allowing it to be tasked at different places at differing times, was against the traditional wisdom in the army. This misplaced quest for under command has been and will forever be, the underlying cause of discontent between armies, navies and air forces in operational matters.

---

[3] Ibid p. 10.

While professional education will mitigate the misunderstanding, the human nature will always ensure that the seeds of discontent are preserved and flower under adversity. As we review the history of joint warfare in 20th century, we will notice the presence of the above factor repeatedly, including the latest wars, where air power has dominated the warfare, most predominantly.

Resuming the history of USAF, post Vietnam experience, the lessons of Yom Kippur War of Oct 1973 and to counter the over whelming follow-on forces of the Warsaw Pact in Europe, the US Army and the Air Force evolved towards closer doctrinal understanding. The US Army 'Air Land Battle' doctrine was embraced by the USAF. "The new manuals addressed the concept of joint operations and the concept that mutually supporting air and ground operations, to include air interdiction, counter air operations, reconnaissance and ground operations are best directed by air commander".[4] In 1990 the two services published a white paper, titled, "Air Attack on modern Battle Field" which led to the development of the five part Air Attack action plan. The Air Attack Action plan synchronized joint air attack combat planning and procedures. The next revision was to the Air Force tactical air control system – Army air ground system, or TACS- AAGS which was modernised, tested and validated in exercises during 1990. Finally, a tactics, technique and procedures manual on joint Air Attack Team (JAAT) procedures was updated and published in October 1991, providing for the integrated use of helicopter, close air support aircraft and field artillery".[5]

Talking about air support in current times, the USAF doctrine AFDD – 2-1.3 states "..CAS also tends to be less efficient use of aerospace power than AI, due to its localised effects, the tactical disposition of enemy targets, and the added restrictions when attacking in close proximity to friendly ground forces.[6]" It further explains that while GPS guided JDAMS can hit stationary targets 24 hours a day and in all weather, the question of target co-ordinate accuracy and guidance reliability will have to be answered to

---

4. Lee,Ibid p. 33.

5. Lee, Ibid.p. 4

6. AFDD. Counter Land Operations, 27 Aug 1999 2-1.3.pp. 2-4.

both the air and ground components' satisfaction, before this option is used.

It is well known that modern battles are mobile and manoeuvre battles. As yet there is no fool proof, air delivered weapon against mobile targets. What we see as Drone attacks on individual mobile targets are far different than immediate CAS missions in a live battlefield. The fratricide casualties in the Iraq War of 91 and since then, are more a result of passing wrong target co-ordinates to aircraft, latest technology and previous training not withstanding. It is an important issue to decide benefits of frequent immediate CAS.

To put it another way, in an environment where militaries are not involved in intense war, CAS against individuals and even mobile target must be pursued. In such a case, all the available infrastructure can be orchestrated towards such elusive targets, without the worry about parallel, competing demands from others. But in an intense conventional war, the demands of frequent CAS may impose rather strict restrictions on other weapons of fire support. These could otherwise be used to good effect.

United-Kingdom

Air Power in UK began as air arms of the Army and Navy. The experience in the earlier part of World War I for air support of the Army, as well as organising air defence of UK against German Zeppelin air ships and Gotha Bombers, compelled the British, to reorganise the two air arms. Thus, in 1917 Royal Flying Corps, an independent service came into being. It was the direct result of the need to centralize control of air assets, for best utilisation. This led to excellent army air support, towards the closing stages of World War I.

During the Inter War years, the strategic bombing debate overshadowed every other facet of air warfare in United Kingdom also. However, unlike the US, in UK, air defence evolved as a coherent, centralized activity, notably supported by technology. This, by way of acoustic sensors to locate hostile aircraft, powerful search lights, to illuminate enemy bombers during night, anti aircraft artillery, balloon barrages, observers with binoculars and last but the most important RADAR. Nurtured, patronised and organised by Air

Marshal Sir Hugh Dowding, the Air defence model of RAF would be copied by all other Air Forces, in years to come. It would be the last bastion of defence against the German bomber offensive, which saved the day for UK and thus the Allies. Unfortunately, the air support of the Army got neglected, doctrinally, equipment wise, procedures as well as training wise. "In September 1939, the British Army and the Royal Air Force did not possess an agreed joint doctrine for integrating air power with the operations of an army in the field. There was no tactical air force for working closely with an army and there was no joint system of command and communications. There were no suitable attack aircraft flexible enough to engage a range of targets at or near the battle front, or survivable enough to defend themselves against hostile aircraft. In short, the British Army and Royal Air Force had no air land capability for modern war."[7] Thus, ill trained British Expeditionary force in France, faced with the lightning German armour advance, the Blitzkrieg, was totally routed. Its air support squadrons, inferior in performance, training, available air intelligence etc. were shot out of the sky. Trying to destroy German bridge head at Mesues River, crossing on 14 May 1940, RAF lost 44 aircrafts from 72 sorties, on this day alone. It was a self destruct attrition rate of 62%.[8] The French had been defeated mentally and bypassed on the ground. The British were defeated too, but managed to escape the German noose at Dunkirk, largely due to RAF not allowing German Luftwaffe air superiority over Dunkirk. But alas, there was no visible close air support. Out of these shambles, the British RAF would once again reinvent and reorganise air support for the Army, in the testing grounds of North Africa. The model developed in 1940–41 and perfected under Generals Sir Auchinleck, succeeded by Montgomery and Air Marshal Tedder, with Air Vice Marshal Conningham, in 1941-42, would become the template for army air support, for future decades. In early 1943, the basic principles were promulgated under General Montgomery's direction, which remains valid even today.

---

[7] Ian Gooderson, "The British Air-Land Experience in the Second World War," Air Power Review, Autumn 2006.p.1.

[8] Gp Capt Alistair Byford, "Combined and Joint Lessons," Air Power Review, Summer 2008, p.61.

- The first requirement for any major land operation was air superiority.

- Flexibility and the capacity for rapid concentration, constituted the main strength of air power

- Control of air power must therefore be centralized in an air commander and exercised through air force channels.

- Air Force must be concentrated and not dispersed in 'penny packets'.

- The Army and Air Commanders and their staff must work closely together.

- The plan of operations must be joint from the start, and mutually adjusted.[9]

The initial British strategic bombing had failed. The US strategic bombing suffered severe setback as it was introduced in Europe. Both happened for the lack of 'Command of Air'. It was the continental size overstretch of Hitler, towards the Russian heartland, and the dogged Russian defence, that gave the allies, time to re-learn from mistakes. It gave American industries time to produce necessary weapons of war, including the desperately needed long-range, air superiority fighters.

Before World War II, air power was also used most innovatively in policing the vast British Empire. "RAF was used as an affordable means of controlling the empire, to this end, air control was exercised in Somalia, the Sudan, the Yemen, Jordan, Afghanistan – and Iraq, where 8 squadron replaced 33 battalions of infantry and 6 regiments of cavalry and successfully restored law and order."[10] Post World War II again, RAF would employ itself, in support of army for COIN in Malay, Oman with large success. These lessons have bearing on use of air power in the COIN operation and with suitable adaptations, can be of great help in our internal law and order problem. Charles Trench, an experienced frontier (NWFP) hand recalls: 'So efficient were communications – a carrier pigeon from gasht (Patrol) to

---

[9] Goodersson, Ibid.p.11.

[10] ACM Sir John Allison, AOC-in-C Strike Command RAF, speech at RUSI – Trenchard Memorial Lecture on 24 Nov 98.

fort, then by telephone and radio to Miran Shah – that in this half an hour of calling for help, a gasht could expect a plane overhead.'[11]

Sebastian Cox aptly summed up the British experience of air/land relationship. "There are those who describe the Air/Land relationship as lurching from unmitigated disaster to unsullied triumph. This view tends to see World War I as very good, particularly at the end; the inter war years as poor, the early Second World War period as disastrous, the later war period as very good, and the post-war era as a curate's egg, good or bad in parts according to taste".[12]

The historical examination reveals some further observations, which has a significant role in air/land relationship, in the past and will continue to be so in future.

- The differing military philosophies of the soldiers and the airmen often have greater impact than the process and equipment and air land relationship. The concept of under command but on an as required basis. Only a proper professional, evaluating without any biases, can mitigate this conflicting perception. Training to look at larger/strategic picture before smaller / tactical picture is essential as well. If not understood, it leads to desire of 'apportionment of air assets', resulting in many 'Penney Packets' under many commands. History proves it to be Penney wise & pound foolish.

- Fratricide or blue on blue casualties have remained, despite so many advance-including technological fixes. Rather as air power is becoming increasingly precise, the reducing of collated damage by leaps and bounds, causes the few fratricidal number to add up to rather large portion of our casualties. To a soldier, thus, 'under command," might appear to be the solution with respect to fratricide. Being a two dimensional person, with limited terrestrial vision, it is difficult, if not impossible for him to visualise the scene from the

---

[11] Maj Andrew Roe, "Air Power on the North-West Frontier of India," *Air Power Review*, Summer 2008. p.38.

[12] Sebastian Cox. "The Air / Land Relationship – a Historical Perspective 1918 – 1991," *Air Power Review*, Summer 2008. p.1.

pilot's perch, in a fast moving aeroplane, looking down upon a vast expanse – wherein everything looks similar. And today, with precise weapons in use, it is the human mistake of passing wrong target co-ordinates, that is responsible for nearly all blue on blue causalities.

The communication revolution has made today's world 'flat' and interconnected instantly. While this is undoubtedly excellent for passing target pictures in real time to the shooter – it is only a part solution to compensate the physical separation between air and land commanders and their staff. This perception of eliminating physical separation is an illusion. What two commanders, face to face and probably with a drink in hand, can achieve, in mutual understanding and adjustment, cannot be achieved in any other way. Ideally, both air and land commanders must be physically together. There is no substitute to this – communication revolution not withstanding.

These observations are valid to all the militaries and the failure to observe them, has continued to produce friction and dissonance, whether it was Gulf War 1991, Iraq War 2003, Kosovo, Afghanistan etc.

Indian Air Force: Policing Role In NWFP

The Indian Air Force, formed on 1ˢᵗ Apr 1933, undertook its first operational task in 1938, when No.1 Flight was sent to NWFP (Miranshah) for air policing work. This new concept of utilising the Air Force was developed by the RAF under Lord Trenchard. At the end of World War I, Britain was in a dire financial position. Yet it faced an increasing burden in imperial commitments, which required more and more ground troops–something Britain could not afford.

At the war's end in 1918, the (British) troops deployed in Iraq, numbered 420 thousand, reducing rapidly on demobilisation. But the post war garrison strength remained high: 25 thousand British and 80 thousand Indian troops, costing at least 18 million pounds a year, to sustain. The serious, but ultimately unsuccessful uprising in 1920, cost 2,300 British casualties and over 8000 Iraq causalities in just three months. Churchill turned to the RAF and asked if they could 'take Mesopotamia on' for uplift in the Air estimate of 5 million pounds ... just over a quarter of 'land heavy' option. In 1922, the RAF took overall command of the policing duties, with a force comprising 8 RAF squadrons, and a mixed army formation of just 2 British and 2 Indian Army brigades. By 1929, a more peaceable Iraq, with a less belligerent Turkey on its border, remained. CAS–Air Marshal John Salmond was the first commander of this joint force, in 1922. He noted, "... No action is ever taken except at the request of the British civilian adviser on the spot, and only after his request has been duly weighed by the (Iraq) Minister of Interior and by the British Adviser and by the High Commissioner (in Baghdad). Even after a request has passed this three – fold scrutiny, I have on more than one occasion, as the High Commissioner's Chief Military Adviser, opposed it on the military grounds, that I did not consider that the offensive action which I had been asked to take, would lead to the result desired..."

Air Marshal Sir John Slessor, an RAF officer and thinker during those times, observed that use of air for policing had resulted in lesser casualties on both sides. He also stressed the point that far from acting in splendid isolation, aircrafts were used extensively, in direct co-operation with land forces; in reconnaissance duties; patrolling convoys; photographic survey and map-making; civilian evacuation; medical re-supply and evacuation; anti-slavery patrols; famine relief; fishery protection; troop transport; and the development of air routes.[13]

France

The French emerged from World War I, victorious but highly distraught. The economy had been shattered. The flower of the French manpower had been sacrificed at the 500 mile long trench warfare altar. The declining birth rate left an awful gap in comparative manpower. As an example from the class of 1915, the French had just 1,84,000 available for conscription as against 4,64,000 for Germany.[14]

The French perceived the next war, sooner than later, to be of static

---

[13] Extracted from Lecture to the Royal Aeronautical Society 2009 by Chief of Air Staff, Air Chief Marshal Sir Stephan Dalton KGB ADC BSC FRAeS CCMI RAF

[14] Alistair Byford, Ibid.p.61.

nature similar to World War I. The armoured tanks' appearance during World War I in 1917 had signalled an end to static warfare. Similarly, the ability of Air Force to hit targets, beyond the frontline, defined success in 1918. Yet the French remained wedded to the idea of linear, slow moving fronts. Hence a major portion of defence spending was towards creating the 'Maginot Line," as fortified linear defence along the Franco – German border. In its conception and execution it was magnificent. It led to a strong belief that Maginot line defence was impenetrable and the French could be rest assured of security from any invasion. The few gaps in Maginot line, towards North, across Belgium and in the mountainous terrain of Ardennes would be defended by small mobile forces and reservists. As the battle progressed–more forces would reinforce the invasion area.

The French Air Force (L' Armee de l' Air) had achieved independent status in 1933. However, unlike the USA and UK, where strategic bomber debate shaped Air forces, in France, the Air Force was a junior partner of the Army, concentrating mainly on reconnaissance and screening of small forces. Though centrality of obtaining and maintaining air superiority had not been forgotten, in defence prioritization it was relegated. The command control structure remained highly hierarchical/stove piped. The Air Force was parcelled out between Army commanders in 'Under Command' fashion. Centralized command, to flexibly concentrate at points of crises/decision was given a back seat.

Thus, so prepared, the French faced the German blitzkrieg. Germans, as we will see later, operated the Luftwaffe in parallel roles, simultaneously. The roles were to obtain air superiority, to interdict, to Para drop, and to support the army battle. Post World War II, the French utilised air power in the former colony of Indo China/Vietnam. But over reliance on air maintenance of troops and use of combat air, without adequate ground security of operating base at Dien Bien Phu, resulted in a catastrophic defeat, leading to the end of the French rule. Algerian insurgency in 1954 – 1962 too, saw French use of combat air in COIN role, successful though somewhat un-refined and brutal application of combat air. Though the French have continued to remain at the forefront of civil and military aviation, their forces have not been tested seriously in conflicts, during the last 50 years.

Germany

Germany lost World War I psychologically, due to inept political leadership. Germany was still occupying French and Belgian territories at the time of accepting defeat. Post World War I Germany still had plenty of professional military personnel, seeking to redeem the World War I defeat and avenge the humiliation of the Treaty of Versailles.

In the cloak of civil commercial aviation, Germany continued to evolve the concept of combat aviation. After Hitler's rise to power in 1933, the German rearmament programme began in a serious manner. While General Weaver was reorganising aviation and the Luftwaffe in a systemic manner, the German Army was experimenting with mobile warfare, centred around armoured thrusts. The role and part of Luftwaffe, in this mobile warfare was tried out. The blitzkrieg success of German war machines was attributed mainly to rapid manoeuvres, by German armoured formations, supported exceedingly well by the Luftwaffe. Therefore, it would be worthwhile to study the genesis of Army – Air support in Germany. Like their counterparts in USA, UK, etc., the task of army – air support had last priority in initial Luftwaffe thinking. Then came the Spanish Civil War in 1936. Hitler willingly provided substantial aid to rebels, especially in aircrafts. Spain became the testing ground for Luftwaffe's concepts and aircrafts.

Wolfram Von Richthofen, Chief of Staff to the Condor Legion (German forces) recognised that the theories of airpower and Spanish political realities did not have much in common. The stalemate on the ground, the lack of suitable "strategic" targets and the weakness in artillery for Nationalist forces (being supported by the Germans) led Richthofen to consider using his air force, to support directly, the Nationalists' offensive.

Against considerable opposition and without official sanction, Richthofen developed the technique and tactics of close air support for ground forces in offensive operations. None of the elements required for such operations existed within the Luftwaffe, before the offensive against the Basque Republic. To begin with, there was an overall lack of experience and technical expertise, for communication between the ground and air units(radio communication) did not yet exist. By the time Richthofen was through developing the concepts and tactics, the Germans had recognised the necessity for close cooperation and improved planning between ground and air units, had established close communication links and recognition devices, and had detailed Luftwaffe liaison officers, to serve directly with frontline units. These liaison officers communicated with CAS aircraft pilots describing targets. The system, when working at its peak, could provide CAS aircrafts within 10 – 20 minutes. All of this was due to Richthofen's drive and imagination[15]. However, the Chief of Staff, Jeschonnek, emphasised the vulnerability of the CAS aircraft and was concerned about the attrition rates that could be expected, particularly if air superiority was not assured. He ordered that CAS was only to be undertaken, where there was likely to be a high pay – off. So despite popular perception of the Luftwaffe being used as aerial artillery, direct air support of ground forces was a comparative rarity in the Polish campaign and this remained the case in France.[16]

Spain also indicated the difficulties of hitting targets by both day and night. The problem of hitting targets accurately in day light missions, helped push Udet towards his conception that every bomber should have a dive bombing capability.[17]

As far as the rest of the roles of air power, strategic bombing being the most important, in Germany, ground realities shaped the overall concepts. Unlike the USA and UK, both guarded by oceans and seas, Germany was primarily a continental country with hostile France to the West, Poland in North East and Czechoslovakia to the east. Here, wars, once started would be decided by ground battles, without enough time or opportunity to try out the concept of strategic bombing, by itself winning the war.

The result of this strategic reality was that Luftwaffe tied its plan for

---

[15] Williamson Murray, "Strategy for Defeat – the Luftwaffe 1933 – 1945," Air University, Alabama, USA, 1983, p.15

[16] Alistair Byford, Ibid, p.65

[17] Ibid p.16

both 1938 and 1939, closely to the operations of the Army. The tasks of the two air fleets, assigned to support the invasion of Czechoslovakia, were to destroy the Czech Air Force, to hinder the mobilisation and movement of reserves, to support the Army's advance, and only then to attack the enemy populations. We shall see this concept of operations repeatedly in all campaigns[18].

So on the eve of World War II, Luftwaffe had been organised and equipped for the following. It had a large aircraft inventory to enable simultaneous operations for air superiority, battlefield interdiction in support of army, air interdiction by bombers and special operations, using paratroops.

It achieved air superiority in the initial few days in campaign against Poland, France and Soviet Union. Simultaneously, its bombers undertook air - interdiction and battlefield air interdiction. It had dedicated air defence of key points/bridge heads by fighters as well as ground based anti- aircraft artillery. Its paratroopers, para dropped at key airfields, key bridges and defensive forts, captured these choke points to enable planned rapid thrusts of German armour. It's dedicated aircraft for reconnaissance for Army provided fast situational updates for ground commanders, to blunt the limited counter attack, launched by the British expeditionary force. The Stuka dive bombers, fitted with air wailing sirens caused immense psychological pressure on ground troops, along with accurate air support.

It was only the Air Defence Command of RAF, while defending Dunkirk and later British homeland that offered serious opposition to Luftwaffe. Luftwaffe lost the battle of Britain to RAF, mainly due to it's centralized air defence but also including many other additional reasons. Hence, what is important to realise is that Luftwaffe conceptually and doctrinally, had been built upon solid foundation, that resulted in lightning success initially.

The battle of France was characterised by the German Army and Luftwaffe's ability to use effective joint tactical doctrine to concentrate forces. Their plans were crafted jointly and executed in an orchestrated manner. As an example, successful crossing of Meuse River at Sedan by

---

[18] Ibid p.19.

the Germans was essential to establish a bridge head. Then from this bridge head, the armoured thrust was to be launched by three Panzer divisions. The Luftwaffe supported the above operation by dedicating the whole of VII Fliegeskerps. But this air support was not like the immediate air support at the active front, as (mis) perceived by most. Rather the air effort was directed, in a concentrated manner at selected critical points. While the bridge head was being established, the French positions around the area were constantly bombarded by relays of strike aircraft to keep them pinned down and minimise their opposition to the German build up. For this, Luftwaffe flew around 800 sorties. Local air superiority had been obtained here.

The Ally's response here was sporadic, piecemeal and delayed. It was piecemeal because the French and British air forces were/could not be used in a concentrated manner. Their response was delayed due to rather long and hierarchical communication chains, for seeking air support. The British often had to ring up London, who would in turn direct the RAF expeditionary squadrons in France. Added to this was the rapid German advance, wherein RAF air bases kept regularly falling into German hands and ruined the RAF's attempt at orderly retreat. It was the absence of timely centralized control that robbed the Allied Air Force's flexibility to concentrate in time and space.

The psychological terror of screaming air sirens fitted on Stukas over French soldiers was tremendous in shattering their morale. Long after Stukas had expanded their armament, their dummy dives passing only with air sirens seemed equally effective. In addition, the Germans quickly deployed 200 anti- aircraft guns around the bridge head and outflew the Allied Air effort nearly four times. Luftwaffe flew 814 sorties against 250 Allied sorties.[19]

In Germany, the Luftwaffe was never controlled directly by the Army. Instead it was concentrated under centralized control for specific missions as part of an integrated air – land battle plan. This plan centred an attaining air superiority and in parallel, isolating the battlefield and cutting lines of communication as understood by battlefield air interdictions. Integrating close

---

[19] Alistair Byford, Ibid, p.67

air support was best avoided, except in emergent situations like when the British forces under Lord Gort, in their counter attack, tried to cut the Germans' advance towards Dunkirk. When Luftwaffe ignored these principles, it too suffered heavily. For example, on May 12, a squadron of strikes lost 16 aircrafts to just five French fighters, when it was caught without its fighter escort.[20]

In our environment and its geographical realities, combined with our reluctance (fortunately) for total war, the Luftwaffe model, as created for World War II, appears most appealing. This should remain an important consideration when we come to command and control for modern times.

---

[20] Ibid p 69.

3

THE MODERN WORLD – FLAT ARCHITECTURE

" *Printing was invented in China in the eighth century AD and movable type in the eleventh century, but this technology only reached Europe in the fifteenth century. Paper was introduced into China in the second century AD, came to Japan in the seventh century, and was diffused westward to Central Asia in the eighth century, North Africa in the tenth, Spain in the twelfth, and northern Europe in the thirteenth. Another Chinese invention, gunpowder, made in the ninth century, disseminated to the Arabs a few hundred years later and reached Europe in the fourteenth century.*"

Samuel P. Huntington

"The 21ˢᵗ Century will be the century of change. More things will change in more places in the next 10 years than in the previous 100. Most countries aren't ready for this dizzying ride – certainly not the United States of America"

Fareed Zakaria

Since the beginning of human civilization, new ideas, innovations, discoveries and processes have continued to enrich the human life, increase overall prosperity and security. The rate of growth too, has continued to evolve starting from humble beginnings. The renaissance in medieval Europe, the printing press, the steam engine in various machines, have all accelerated this process of change. In the 20th century, the creation of microchip and computing power, along with global connectivity has brought about a revolutionary change that is unprecedented.

Table : Rate of Change

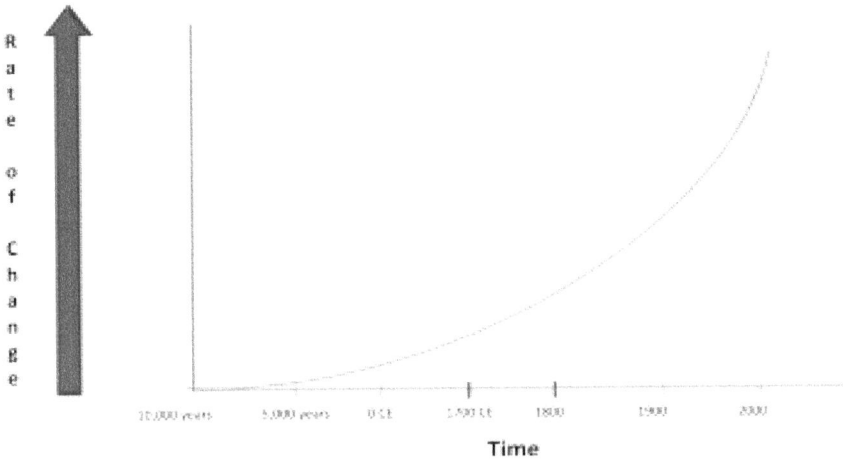

Moore's law tells us that every 18 – 24 months, the computing growth of a chip will double. Conversely it has also been realised that as the computing power doubles, the cost comes down by nearly half. It was thought that Moore's law will come to a blind ally as we reach the physical limit in chip manufacturing ability. That is, the physical size of chip will limit the ultimate number of circuits possible on it. However, the developments in nano- technology and quantum computing are akin to breaking the sound barrier. This means that Moore's Law will continue to hold good till we reach nano limits of an atom – a very distant limit. This has resulted in a world, which is quite different even from the previous century. The main game changers are:

1. The fibre optic cables laid across the world, along with ever increasing number of satellites with ever increasing capacity and marvels of digitisation which will make flow of unlimited data across the world at the speed of light. To access this data, however, one would need to be connected to this global net by a suitable device. Earlier this device was a high end computer. Today, hand held devices like the ubiquitous mobile phone, suffice.

2. Today phenomenally voluminous data can be processed in seconds,

25

provided one has suitable software for the same. The information, translated into knowledge can enable decision making real fast – in seconds and minutes. Without suitable software it can so overload a system that the system itself is paralysed.

3.   The same extensive network allows execution of quick decision making equally quickly by various responsible agencies /platforms. The era of live sensor to shooter has arrived. That is, the Observe, Orient, Decide and Act cycle of Col Boyd is now reduced to near real time. The same capability and process applied across other fields of economy, manufacturing, services etc have increased efficiencies and productivity to the levels never seen in the past.

The next fundamentally important change is the certainty of knowing our physical positions, very accurately in four dimensions. The GPS allows a person equipped with suitable receiver to know his two dimensional positions within units of metres, his vertical position within tens of metres and the prevailing time to nano second accuracy. This, coupled with augmented GPS system, improves the accuracy to sub- metre figures. For millennia in the past, people were unsure of their position – the most famous being Columbus. Today, one knows one's own position most precisely. Also one knows the enemy's position precisely, with the help of multiple types of sensors – onboard satellites, onboard aircrafts and UAVs as well as hand held sensors, provided the enemy can be seen. Unless hidden underground, the sensors can spot by day and night, in clouds and rain, in fog and smog, in dust and sand, albeit with some limitations. The sensors to look underground and within deep foliage are also under development.

To top it all now we have weapons equipped with GPS receivers and / or other sensors with sophisticated software. These weapons can be guided to any set of target co-ordinates, fed into the system. The accuracy of such weapons is the accuracy of coordinates entered. The few limitations existing in them will be elaborated later for each type of weapon.

This transformed world has made global economy seem local. Chinese goods of every variety are everywhere – and highly cost effective. The volume of global trade by sea, rail, road and air enables items made in one continent to reach another, making it easy and competitive.

The world wide media coverage generates global interests in happenings world wide. As anyone can enjoy sports, events and shows staged all around the world at the press of TV button, one also becomes aware of sufferings and atrocities, globally. The human empathy has acquired global connection. Human rights evoke global response. The world today is far more interconnected economically, and emotionally than ever before.

Another feature of the transformed world is mass participative approach. Swaminathan S Anklesaria Aiyar writing in The Times of India stated, "In the 1990s, the government (GoI) deregulated industry, gradually deregulated finance, and improved the infrastructure for global connectivity. This produced an explosion of ideas and companies that no strategy had even envisaged"[1]. The transformed world finds its echoes in warfare also. The modern battlefield and warfare is also an extremely complex system of systems. It requires willing and timely participation of large number of participants for it to function at its best. The efficiency and effectiveness of this complex web increases incrementally at various levels – the sum total of which produces results far greater than the sum of individual incremental improvements. For such a living system to continuously evolve – it is but essential to "deregulate" enough for each participant. Software enables operation of complex systems. These kinds of software constantly evolve with regular usage, timely feedback, due corrections, further trials and feedback. So we have Microsoft coming out with newer versions of "Windows" regularly. The software of complex military systems can only evolve if it is decentralized and encouraged for constant feed back from participants. This new concept is contrary to what prevailed earlier, wherein leaders decided how and why and juniors followed it to the letter. Now the services need to adapt this participative approach, to constantly evolve the system software. Moreover it is the younger lot vis-à-vis the seniors who are more at home with modern hardware and software. It is their knowledge that alone can produce improvements.

---

[1] *Times Of India,* 08 Jul 2007

Realising the power of participative approach, even the Ministry of External Affairs quickly followed suit. "MEA is bringing foreign policy, so far the subject of closed – door deliberations, privy to a select few, into the public domain. In other words, it plans to involve the civil society in the formulation of our foreign policy. Pranab Mukerjee (Minister of External Affairs) has already taken the first step in this direction, by creating a public diplomacy division within the ministry. It's task is to engage in a dialogue with members of academia, NGOs, industry representatives and media and give shape to policy on the basis of their opinions,"[2]

The Wiki software is reforming isolated bureaucracies and changing the face of communication – reports Jessica Bennete.[3] Wiki software, easy to use programme, that lets anyone with internet access create, remove and edit context on a web page – first gained popularity thanks to Wikipedia, the user generated encyclopedia, that has come to be hailed as one of the web's greatest resources. Now the technology is increasingly spreading outside the world of tech geeks and into mainstream, being adopted by workplaces, corporations and even governments. In what has been dubbed the 'Wiki workplace", a growing number of organisations have begun shifting from traditional hierarchical structures to self – organised and collaborative networks using wiki software – a basket of technologies that include wikis, blogs and other tools, to faster innovation across organisational and geographic boundaries.

The Wiki software can be easily seen on secure networks. In IBM more than 100,000 employees use the Wiki software for updating product documentation and modifying company policies. Sixteen U.S. intelligence agencies have begun using a common wiki called Intelpedia, a government run and top secret – information sharing source that allows them to merge research and intelligence gathering.

The flatter structure of organisations is a result of good connectivity. The globe is very well connected today with extensive amount of fibre optic

---

[2] *Asian Age,* 05 Aug 2007.
[3] *Newsweek,* 06 Aug 2007, pp. 48-49.

cables and commercial satellites. This global expressway allows internet connections of very high speed. For example in Sweden, internet speed of 40 Gbs/sec allows people to download a movie in two seconds. The newer PCs /laptops / tablets/mobiles come equipped with processing power, allowing all the functions. Moore's law predicts the micro chips' capacity to double, every 18 – 24 months. This would continue to double the processing power, while halving the size every two years or so. The latest material created, Graphane is one atom thick. It promises its revolutionary application in chip making as well as in other materials. And it is many times stronger than steel.

Digitisation at every level and source is making the interconnectedness accessible to all people who are connected. Interoperable software, earlier non-existent, now can connect more and more systems together. Open source Linux software, with collaborative approach is as powerful, if not more, as Microsoft. Wikipedia and Wiki sourcing are making every person a genius. Enterprise Resource Planning is providing intelligent output in minutes, solving complex interrelated issues. Earlier these solutions took days and weeks and yet output suffered in accuracy.

These accelerating changes have dawned a new era of globalisation. The global connection, 2000 years back was by the silk route which traded limited numbers of luxury goods, meant only for the kings and like. The globalisation of the industrial age was mainly colonial. The Portuguese, Spanish, French, Dutch and the British established colonies worldwide. They plundered the raw material and colonial wealth; manufactured at homeland, and sold the produce back in captive colonial markets. But amongst the colonising powers, little economic interdependence existed. Therefore, this era was full of inter-state wars, culminating in the two World Wars.

The latest globalisation, post the Cold War era, is markedly different, which has different security implications. Today, massive and voluminous trade moves by sea, rail, road and air globally. Global interconnectedness by Blogs, Youtube, Facebook, My Space, and various search engines along with digitations all over has kindled human interest, in affairs in every corner of the world. In 1800, there were only two democracies. In 1972 there were 40. As of now there are 123 democracies. The Arab world is in turmoil seeking democratic reforms. This means that much more global interest and participation. Thomas Friedman observed, "When every one has a blog, a My Space page or Facebook entry, everyone is a publisher. When everyone has a cell phone with a camera in it, everyone is a paparazzo. When everyone can upload videos on Youtube, everyone is a filmmaker."

Today most of the MNCs have their plants and R&D centres, spread worldwide. There is extensive movement of energy producing raw materials i.e., Oil, Natural gas and Coal worldwide. Parts, components and sub-assemblies produced in different countries, often continents apart, move just in time, to produce many complex products. Boeing and Airbus commercial aircrafts are apt examples. Money flows globally to earn quick bucks in financial markets as well as is invested aboard, for medium to long terms.

This makes today's world highly interdependent economically, unlike the economic autarky till the 19th century. It weakens the traditional concept of political rivalry, easily spilling over into conflict, in case of differences. While all the states try to maximise their POWER, they also realise that POWER based on PLENTY is only possible through global economic co-operation, opines Ashley Tellis. This reduces the chances of classic conventional wars. This is an important security derivative from contemporary globalisation.

How does it affect national decision making? The freedom to pursue simple and clear strategic policies are drastically reduced. Perforce, national strategies will be complex and ambiguous – a result of dynamic interplay of many variables. So the military leadership would be unlikely to get clear cut security mandates. Militaries, therefore, must have flexibility in their doctrine, their force structure, in their campaign planning and in its execution. This is the most important consideration I wish to highlight, before we proceed on our deliberations of reorganisation.

In the transformed world what are the chances of regular wars? What will be the likely shape of conflicts? The table below shows the likelihood of war across various spectrums, in a relative manner. The percentage numbers are only illustrative.

LIKELY HOOD OF WAR ACROSS SPECTRUM

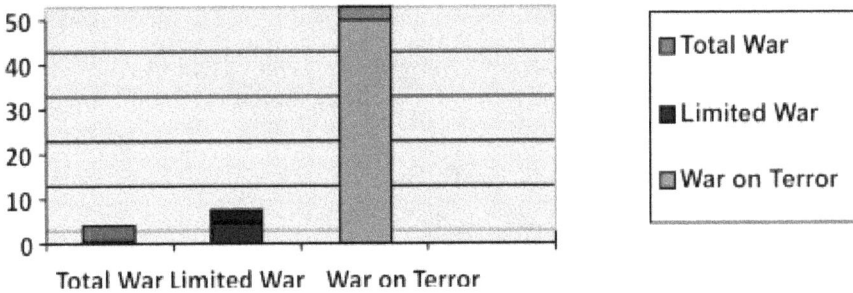

Total War Limited War   War on Terror

The next table below shows the various roles that the air power would be tasked with and their likely chances of execution in future wars. This is an essential step for force structure planning; dual use capability in equipment and building in flexibility in operational structures. Since air power is most expensive, ideally we should be able to switch over smoothly from one spectrum of war to another, as per need with the same equipment and organisation. It would be most unwise to create two types of air force for two different spectrums of war.

Roles & Likelihood – Air Ops

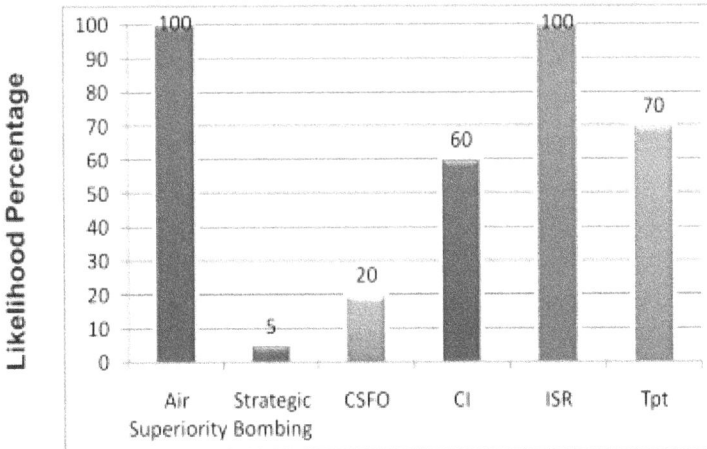

Notes: 1. Air Superiority seldom required for CI Ops.
           2. Air Superiority below 13000' - not achievable.

31

Though air superiority remains the fundamental requirement for all operations, it seldom needs to be established and sustained for CI operations. Air Superiority below 13000 feet, cannot be established in the presence of manual anti aircraft artillery and shoulder launched anti aircraft missiles. The effort to do so would be futile and of unsustainable attrition. In all out conventional wars, strategic bombing occupies the centre stage and rightly so. But if in our scenario, chances of all out conventional wars are extremely limited compared to CI operations and CSFO, then definitely we need to apply our attention proportionately to these operations. The latter has not received due attention in the past due to over attention given to conventional war planning.

A word of caution must be put in about likely roles. Strategic strikes' likelihood indeed would be much lesser in future. But this does not mean it's importance and centrality in conventional warfare would also reduce. If anything, it's ability to destroy key targets would be even more. What will change is the amount of effort or the number of sorties per target. Indeed it will be possible to destroy multiple targets in each sortie. This is a direct result of extremely enhanced ISR and precise weapons. Thus surgical strikes will contribute significantly towards achieving national goals, by destruction of visible and identifiable targets. Even in war on terror, surgical strikes will serve a large purpose.

The above two tables clearly bring out increasing attention towards war on terror and war against insurgents, militants and terrorists. Air forces are primarily configured for conventional wars. And rightly so. But they need to be flexible enough to also undertake war on terror while not compromising the basic conventional capability. Or better still, they must have multitasking capability in equipment, personnel, doctrine and training. In the past on many occasions, many air forces did this when directed for counter insurgency tasks. Some succeeded admirably while some others failed. RAF was successful during inter-war years in Middle East, in Malaysia from 1948 to 1960, and in Kenya from 1952 to 1960. Its record in Northern Ireland during the latter half of last century was mixed. The Israeli Air Force against People's Liberation Army during the 70s and during Intifada in Palestine in the recent past has been successful. The USAF in Iraq and

Afghanistan, in this decade has been quite successful. The French in Algeria from 1954 to 1962 did win the battle though brutally, therefore, losing the war politically and had to move out. In Indo-China from 1946 to 1954, the French lost the main battle despite absolute air superiority and thus politically. Mis- application of air power was a contributory factor. In Vietnam, the US did not lose any battle, thanks to air power. But brutal and indiscriminate application of air power cost them the political war and they had to move out of Vietnam. Soviets suffered similar fate in Afghanistan in 1980s.

This raises an interesting question about suitability of air power in counter-insurgency or for that matter for internal security. Obviously the answer cannot be a simple yes or no. It is complex. It is yes, provided many inter-related factors have been addressed correctly. Failure to do so leads to overall failure even though air power might give tactical victory. With increasing need for internal security in India, there is an urgent need to re-examine the use of air power in this role when, moreover, current technological advances have made today's air power far more effective than it was in the past. What follows is a brief examination.[4]

Generally when one talks of air power and internal security, the critics straightaway jump to the idea of indiscriminate combat application of air power and therefore oppose it vehemently. But air power is much more than only combat power. In difficult terrain, air transportation, including helicopters, in a way multiplies the number of counter insurgent personnel by an order of magnitude. Air transportation also takes away the time and surprise element of the insurgents. One must remember that surprise is the foundation on which insurgents' success rests. Air surveillance reduces the freedom of movement of insurgents. ISR capability by day and night shrinks the freedom envelope of insurgents tremendously. Whether the airborne aircraft/UAV picks up the insurgents or not, as far as the insurgent is concerned he has been exposed. He can not afford to think otherwise. This is a psychological battle in which only air power can enable victory each and every time. Communication relay, prompt casualty evacuation, aerial

---

[4] For detailed examination refer, " Air Power and Counter Insurgency," Lancer Books, Delhi 2002 by same author.

command post etc. are additional roles which enable good counter insurgency campaigns.

As for as combat application of air power, the following needs to be considered. First and foremost, insurgents waging war against the state and its innocent citizens, are enemies of the state. They need to be dealt with as such. Hence violence against them, whether by police, para military force, army or air force is justified. The state has a right to choose the most optimum option. The precise nature of modern air delivered fire power enables selective application of fire against insurgents, with little collateral damage to innocents nearby. Non lethal weapons are opening up another option to be exploited by air power. Thus a modern air force equipped correctly, with suitable doctrine and training can enable internal security duties very effectively.

Apart from the implications for force structure, command and control structure and SOPs for above roles, following additional points also need careful consideration. To defend our island territories and areas beyond, we will have to resort to expeditionary models for air operations. So a modular and mobile structure for command control would be essential. During the Kargil operations of 1999, Srinagar acted as a mini air operations centre for aircrafts in the valley. For aircrafts outside the valley, operations were conducted from HQ WAC. This dual operations centre approach was an on the spot innovation to an emergent unfolding situation in which we were totally surprised. Therefore in the future, we ought to be better prepared.

The next observation is that our command and control structure was created for a conventional war on our western borders. The war time functioning is substantially different from the peace time routine. We expect conventional wars to be of short duration and augment manpower from training establishments. This is possible because we expect sufficient warning time before war. However, this arrangement is not suitable for CI operations. For the past two decades, the militants in the J&K have caused situations requiring large scale troop deployment. This large and highly visible deployment of troops has been shrewdly exploited by people for short term political expediency. The air power innovatively used with ground forces, promises to reduce this large footprint on the ground and overcome the problem. At the same time it can further improve our joint operations against militancy. General Karl Eikenbery, Commander Combined Forces Command Afghanistan remarked in 2007, "Without air and space power, 500- 600000 troops would be needed in Afghanistan to achieve the same effects as the 40000 soldiers, sailors and airmen we have here today. Air and Space power provides the asymmetric advantage over the Taliban, such that no matter where they choose to fight, Coalition forces can muster overwhelming fire power in matter of minutes. Moreover, putting 500 – 600000 into the country may achieve the same military effect, but it could have a negative impact on the population; such numbers could appear as an occupying force, rather than a security assistance force. In short, there is no substitute for effective air and space power.'

So why has this not happened in our case? The most obvious reason appears to be unsuitable command and control structure, which is not tailored for quick all around response. The existing SOPs are such that they are unsuitable for fast and timely response. Israel has been dealing with terrorists for decades. Americans have been in Afghanistan for nine years. So how does their system respond fast enough against mobile and fleeting targets? We need to learn from their experience. CI operations are protracted. They demand few but fast responses, interspersed within large periods of inactivity. They need 24 hrs attention. A command and control system which can meet the requirements of both peace time activity and CI operations is what is required. Probably the Israeli system meets this requirement. While it is easy to meet norms of conventional war, the CI operations demand continuous innovation. Air power used unimaginatively will do more damage than good. RAF has been at the forefront of innovative use of airpower since 1920. Yet once again the mantra for RAF in 2010 is "Agile, Adaptable, and Capable'. The nuclear bomber Tornado GR 4 is doing counter – IED, convoy sweep and route sweep missions in Afghanistan. Surely there are lessons in this for us to consider!

That brings us to the next point about learning by evolution. Those days are over when one learnt all about a weapon system in the first few weeks of classroom. Thereafter, he flew and operated relatively simple weapons systems. Today's weapon systems have extremely complex avionics. The fighting organisations are networked by ERP software. These systems require years of study and regular use to understand and master. Mastery gives the confidence and the ability to evolve further and seek a new set of improvements to the software. At the same time, constantly growing processing power of processors in the commercial world, speeds up the software further. So our command and control structure and SOPs must be open ended for growth. They need to be based on wiki type participative software development. More so since younger lots are far more at home with new technology. We must continue to evolve, as will be soon evident when we examine USAF's air operation centre.

4

THE MODERN BATTLE FIELD

"The goal of a war of the future will not be to seize enemy territory but to inflict surgical strikes against sensitive targets. International borders are not violated, large scale use of ground troops and armour is becoming a thing of the past, and the role of strategic aviation is diminished. The traditional nuclear triad is being replaced with non-nuclear high accuracy weapons with different basing modes."

Andrei Kislyakov[1]

One of the major reason for the above presumption is the growing number of democracies and the fact that no wars have been fought between independent nations, with elected government between 1789 and 1941. Again post World War II democratic governments haven't fought a war amongst themselves. In 1800, there were only 2 democracies, and by February 2007, the numbers had gone up to 135. Thus, the reducing chances of conventional inter-state wars.

Another major reason is the role of technology in today's interconnected world. "We often read during the roaring 1990s, that technology and information had been democratised. This is a relatively new phenomenon. In the past, technology helped reinforce centralization and hierarchy. For example, the last great information revolution – in the 1920s involving radio, television, movies, megaphones – had a centralizing effect. It gave the person or group with access to that technology, the power to reach the rest of the society. That's why the first step in a twentieth century coup was to seek

---

[1] "New Wars and Space Weapons," Andrej Kislyakov – in *India Strategic* Jun 2007. pp 40 – 41.

control of the country's television or radio station. But today's information revolution has produced thousands of outlets for news, that make central control impossible and dissent easy. The internet has taken this process another huge step forward, being a system where, in the columnist, Thomas Friedman's words, "everyone is connected but no one is in control."[2]. The Facebook started a revolution in Tunisia in 2011, and the internet in Egypt ending 30 years dictatorship of Hosni Mubarak, within days.

How does the war in Afghanistan relate to above proposition? "So the Afghanistan conflict, while truly path breaking in its use of high – tech weapons such as GPS – guided bombs and Predator unmanned armed aerial vehicles as well as special forces altogether, the Northern Alliance and other Afghan units were needed on the ground to help defeat the Taliban and Al Qaeda. In addition, US forces failed to achieve key objectives in and around Tora Bora by relying too much on air power and local allies. Finally, stabilising Afghanistan, effectively would have required considerable more forces."[3]

How was the 2003 war in Iraq? "Overall, the main pillars of the coalition's success in Iraq – new technology and traditional skill – made for a remarkable set of capabilities. In terms of equipment, of particular note were the all – weather reconnaissance systems, all – weather bombs, and modern communication networks, developed in the last decade... In addition, the competence of American and British troops and their commanders and the excellence of their training were striking. Indeed, old – fashioned equipment such as tanks performed extremely well, the old – fashioned skills of infantry soldiers were very important and overall, the urban combat operations were executed magnificently."[4]

While most of us get focussed on new technology, it often diverts our attention away from innovative applications of traditional resources. Luftwaffe's use of special forces during the Polish and French campaigns was revolutionary. But now in 2003 and 2010, the use of special forces to

---

[2] *Times of India* 27 Jun 2007.

[3] Michael O Hanlon. "Defence Strategy", Brookings Institute, Washington, 2003 p. 33.

[4] Ibid –p. 37.

utilise modern weapons was highly innovative. Michael O' Hanlon writes, "... special operations raids were more impressive than the early air campaigns. Dozen of small special operations teams disrupted Iraqi command and control, seized oil infrastructure, prevented dams from being demolished, and took hold of airfields in regions where scud missiles might have been launched at Israel. Special operations and intelligence units also appear to have disrupted Iraqi lines of communication in Baghdad and else where, perhaps hastening the collapse of Iraqi forces, as the urban fighting began. These operations were done in a brave, creative and effective manner. They also prevented some nightmarish scenarios. And in several places in north and west of Iraq, small teams of special forces helped hold off much larger Iraqi main combat formations, at key moments."[5]

"... Intelligence units also appear to have disrupted Iraqi lines of communication..." This actually means cyber war on the Iraqi command and control network. It had been done in the 1991 Gulf war, as well as much earlier against erstwhile Soviet gas supply, which resulted in the most monumental non – nuclear explosion and fire ever seen from space."[6]

Gen Wesley K. Clark, C-in-C for Kosovo operations in 1999 characterised waging modern wars, of which one important requirement is phenomenal need for intelligence. '... even with the best – intentioned efforts, "precision strike" will need augmentation by "precision acquisitions and identification of targets. We will need specific information in real time. We will need to see underneath clouds and inside buildings. We will want to know whether the men on the tractors and inside the buses are soldiers or civilians. We will want to know who is in the underground facility, civilian or military, families or opposing leaders."[7]

Mr. Vance Coffman, CEO Lockheed Martin Global Inc, while speaking to the Industry forum on 4 May, 2000, predicted the future battlefield. "That future will increasingly be one of information based strategies – including

---

[5] Ibid-p. 34

[6] "At the Abyss-An Insiders History of the Cold War," Thomas C. Reed, Ballantine Books, New York,2004. p. 269

[7] Gen Wesley K. Clark, "Waging Modern War," Public Affairs, New York, 2001, p. 433.

networks that line "sensors and shooters", integration of ever more complex systems, and delivery of all this information to the commanders who need it, whether in national decision making centres, in cockpits, or in the battlefield itself. In other words, the provision of integrated system of sensors, platforms, weapons and knowledge – so called network – centric solutions, will be key products of our industry." Describing the 2003 Iraq war, Thomas C. Reed stated, "In 2003 one air raid destroyed 500 armoured vehicles and artillery pieces in an elite Republican Guard Division. Only infantry with small arms were left to fend for themselves. A surviving POW described the attack. When the bombs hit the tanks, we ran for our cars. When we turned on the ignition, the bombs hit the cars. It was terrible."

These then are the descriptions of modern battle fields, by persons most of whom participated in latest wars and had first hand experiences to narrate. To get a better grasp, let us see some of the important equipment in use in the modern battlefield. While there is a plethora of new equipment and technology within each service, here it is purposely focussed on joint operations for illustration. The equipment and its presentation order is random. In no way does it imply inter – se priority.

PC / Laptops / Tablets

The personal computer or the personal processing devices which have graduated from a desk top PC to a more user-friendly laptop are already giving way to small hand held devices. This decrease in size but increasing storage, memory, processing, and speed will continue to come for quite a while. Graphane transistors, which are one – atom thick will ensure continued applicability of Moore's law. Graphane, being super – strong will also reduce the weight of future aircrafts, satellites and such devices.[8] Such devices, when integrated in the battlefield network will make the network that much more powerful.

Transparency of the Battlefield

A review of ISR sensors shows that in the beginning a sensor was used in

---

[8] *Times Of India,* 06 Oct 2010

isolation. Each sensor had certain limitations, for example EO (electro optic) sensors could see only during day light hours, the targets which reflected light. EO sensors could not see in the darkness or camouflaged targets. Hence alternate sensors like IR, and Thermal sensors were developed which could see in the dark, detecting an object by its heat contrast with the surrounding. The two sensors combined i.e., EO & IR gave a somewhat 24 hours capability. Advances in science and technology are continuing to make sensors which are more effective, yet weigh less and cost less. The smaller size is enabling their use on smaller aircraft and UAVs. This trend will continue. Thus, we already see aerial platforms with multiple sensors. When used in combination, they make more and more of the battle field transparent, revealing more targets that can be engaged. A brief summary of various sensors follows :

- **EO Sensors** : Electro Optic sensors are like cameras with magnifying power.

- **IR Sensors** : These work by seeking heat energy radiated by the target in contrast to its surrounding.

- **Thermal Sensors** : They too work by seeking heat energy of the target, but at different frequencies and wave lengths.

- **Imaging IR Sensors** : These seek targets by this heat emission in a different frequency range.

- **Multi Spectral** : Targets emit radiation / reflect light by different amounts in different wavelength of VIBGYOR and beyond. Sensors which can detect targets, using multi – spectral sensing and synthesize the return, work better than single wavelength sensors. Sensors using multiple windows in narrow bands of wave lengths are characterised as Multi spectral sensors.

- **Hyper Spectral Sensors** : Multi spectral sensors having many sensors in contiguous bands of wavelength sensors are classified as hyper spectral sensors.

- **Ultra Spectral:** Sensors with even more numbers are called Ultra Spectral.

- **Radars** : Sensors which detect reflected energy from a target are called primary radars. A secondary radar detects the transmitted signal from another aircraft.

- **Synthetic Aperture Radar** : Provides pictures of terrain and targets, instead of just dots as in a conventional radar.

- **MTI – Radar** : Radar which distinguishes moving targets in contrast to a static background.

- **Acoustic Sensors:** Sensors which detect sound waves.

A series of modest jumps in various sensors along with suitable data processing algorithms in newer and faster computers will work to produce more enhanced results in reconnaissance and interpretation. The combination of sensors could even enable passive surveillance, where maintaining secrecy is an important issue . The ability to combine radar data with that from IR, visible light, acoustic and other sensors combined with high speed, large memory computers directed by clever new algorithms will enhance reconnaissance, substantially. This should reduce the problems in finding concealed, camouflaged and mobile targets. Target identification can be further enhanced by cross – referencing, by overlaying emissions or communications, such as those from command vehicles or mobile anti-aircraft weapons.

The increasing transparency of the battlefield, combined with a growing number of precise and smart weapons will further reduce the need for a ground controller to direct strike aircraft. In any case, the amount of direction required to indicate the target to a strike aircraft/UAV will definitely not demand the need for a trained fighter pilot to be on ground as an FAC.

SAR (Synthetic Aperture Radar)

SAR technology creates a virtual antenna several hundred metres in width by analysing the Doppler frequency of a series of radar scans, from a moving aircraft. SAR combines the all – weather capability of radars with image resolution of near photographic quality, giving it an advantage over EO and IR systems. Future developments are expected to shrink the total weight of a tactical SAR system to less than 4.5 kg. The EADS Defence and Communication Systems Miniature SAR already weighs less than 4 kg and has a resolution of 50 cm.[9]

Video Pictures' Transmission

Normally transmission of video pictures, which comprises of Gigabytes of data requires lot of bandwidth. However, Glasgow based Essential Viewing appears to have made a revolutionary breakthrough in video compression. The US Navy SEALS are believed to have been the first users of this technology in 2001 in Afghanistan. This method allows video feeds on existing communications' infrastructure. For example, anywhere there is a cellular telephone network, it can be used to transmit video camera imagery. It does not have to be a mobile phone network, it could equally well be a narrow – band satellite or field radio systems. What more, the picture can be received over the Internet by Java – enabled browsers or even latest mobile phones.[10]

There are many companies involved in compressing image data for easy transmission. Treppid Technologies can compress the data by a factor of 400 : 1 with very little perceptible loss of quality. For comparisons, one second's worth of uncompressed full – motion video, running at 30 frames per second, with each frame containing 640 X 480 pixels of 24 bit color information would require 211 Mbit/Sec of communication bandwidth for transmission and 26.4 M bytes for storage capacity. With use of above compression, the same data can be transmitted, using narrow band (56 K bit/Sec) communication links.[11]

However, there are limits. "There is a ground swell of opinion that suggests that solution lies in FMV (full motion video). Receive only Video Enhanced Receiver (ROVER) is in use with several ground units in Iraq giving the predator FMV picture to local commanders. Despite the attraction of 24/7 video, the spell – binding download from predator and other UAVs it is having limited value. As with still images, unless interpreted by an

---

[9] Jane's Defence Weekly, 21 Jul 04, "UAV Payload Developments" pp. 45-49.

[10] Defence News – 18 Aug 03 "Live from Battlefield"

[11] Jane's International Defence Review, Aug 2003, p.24

image analyst, it is often hard to discern the relevance of what one sees. Colour, high – resolution video gives plenty of information but little intelligence because it cannot show intent."[12]

Obtaining technology is easy though costly – sometimes a lot. Where and how to use it are questions that demand impassioned analysis and thorough professionalism. This alone maximises impact of technology, while keeping away unnecessary distraction. Also it makes planning less expensive and more effective.

RPV / UAV / UAS / UCAS

Air vehicles without pilots in the cockpit have been referred to as RPVs in the past. As the potential of RPVs increased, the aviation community endowed them newer names like UAV, UAS, UCAS etc. The fine differentiation applied by the professionals is not so relevant for us as long as we understand UAV to be a system without pilots in the cockpit. For our understanding, a UAV could be big, small or micro in size, could carry one or more sensors in ISR role, could be armed with weapons as circumstances demand, etc. It could be stealthy, ultra high altitude and ultra high endurance. It's roles could expand in the future. For our discussion, we shall not consider the small tactical UAVs carried by individual soldiers, though our solutions will cater to their employment .

When will the manned air forces be replaced by UAVs totally? Probably never. But surely the share of UAVs in future Air Forces will continue to increase, ISR roles being the largest. In weapon delivery role, it depends upon the imagination and opportunities. In other roles too, it is the same, though it might occur more slowly. So let us see the future of UAV in years to come in order to organise properly, for future battle space.

Soon, the UAVs will add the much desired quality of " Persistence," to air power roles, which had remained a major drawback for air power in the first century of flight. These assumptions are supported by the following.

---

[12] Gp Capt R M Poole, " The Utility of Air Power in Nation Building," RAF Air Power Review, Summer 2005, p.17

"The Israeli Air Force (IAF) will dramatically curtail the number of its fighters and by 2030, half of its platforms will be unmanned, according to the IAF's new road map."[13] In 2030, IAF is likely to have 80 F-35; 25 F-15 I; 100 F-16 I and 200 unmanned aircraft. The unmanned system will carry out many of its current missions, including attacks on ground targets. The unmanned systems will consist of multirole long-endurance UAS.

Royal Australian Air Force is considering making 30% of its advanced strike fleet, unmanned.[14] India's ADA as well as DRDO are developing armed UAVs.[15] This programme is separate from other ongoing efforts by the Indian military to integrate weapons on UAVs.

DARPA's (USA) goal is to develop a heavier than air prototype, capable of keeping 1000 lb of payload aloft for five years with 5 kw of power. Work on this capability, which is described as 'pseudo satellite' systems, will run through February 2014, the initial objective being to prove at least 30 days of flight in 2014. The UAV will be based on solar / electric power.[16] The aircraft called Solar Eagle is being built by the Boeing company.

Aerovironment's Global Observer, hydrogen – powered high altitude, long endurance unmanned aircraft is being designed to fly at 55000 – 65000 feet for 5 – 7 days, carrying a 400 lb payload. Two aircrafts would provide continuous coverage.[17]

Stealth will become a standard in UAV fleets just as it is in manned combat aircraft today. This is borne out by the design of Global Hawk, Northrop Grumman's X-47-A & X-47 B etc. The new roles and missions are piling up faster than USAF's UAV equipment and crew. J-UCAS (Joint Unmanned combat air systems) in US will have concurrent roles of ISR, air to ground strike, air to air combat and SEAD, EW, communications interception etc. The predator force alone will jump to 15 squadrons from 3

---

[13] AWST – 6 Sep 2010 "Brave New World" A Ion Ben- David. p. 26.

[14] AWST 27 Mar 06, p. 30

[15] AWST 7 Jun 2010, p. 38

[16] AWST 20/27 Sep 2010. p. 31.

[17] AWST – 31 May 2010. p. 14.

squadrons in the next few years.[18]

Predator B, a follow – on hunter – killer UAV is bigger, faster, flies higher and carries more weapons. Predator Bs are designed to carry 16 Hellfire missiles, six GBU – 12 laser guided 500 lb bombs or four 500 lb GPS guided JDAMs and fly as high as 50000 feet.[19] In fact since the year 2009 onwards, nearly all the strikes against Taliban hiding in the sanctuary of Afghanistan – Pakistan border have been by the UAVs. This clearly illustrates the role and place of UAVs in future. In what could be the largest top secret aircraft programme since B-2 bomber, the USAF is racing to develop a stealthy, supersonic, long range unmanned reconnaissance plane.[20] USAF created multiple mini organisations called Battle Labs after the Gulf War – 91 to pursue desired advances in various technologies. One such was a UAV battle lab. During trials in 2000, the USAF's UAV battle lab successfully demonstrated the military utility of a Situational Awareness Data Link (SADL) radio aboard a Hunter UAV. The objective was to demonstrate the ability to supply UAV position information to attacking fighters and ground forces, and to provide the position of friendly troops equipped with Enhanced Position Location Reporting System (EPLRS) to FAC and the UAV payload operators.

Another UAV battle lab demonstration known as , "Spotter." used a Hunter UAV equipped with an Infrared Zoom Laser Illuminator Designator (12 LID II) to illuminate ground targets for night close air support and air interdiction mission. It was highly successful.[21] High energy laser and high power microwave weapons to fit on UAVs are being investigated by Raytheon, TRW and Lockheed Martins.[22]

This brings us to the key question about command and control of UAVs and their place in battlefield, more so when Indian Air Force, Army and Navy, between themselves, have around ten squadrons of UAVs. In addition

[18] AWST 26 Sep 05 . p. 30.

[19] AWST 30 May 05. p. 51.

[20] Defence News 02 Aug 04.

[21] Jane's International Defence Review, Sept 2002, p. 55.

[22] AWST 25 Feb 2010. p. 28.

other agencies like the Coast Guard and BSF are also planning to induct UAVs. It is estimated that the Indian Air Force itself will increase UAVs' numbers from the present 5 Squadrons to around 17 Squadrons in the next 10-15 years.[23]

Israel engaged in operations 24 hours a day, 7 days a week and has put all aerial platforms operationally, under Israeli Air Force, including all the UAVs. That helps tremendously in command and control, training, equipping, servicing, maintaining and most importantly, operationally.[24] But in most other countries, all three services operate UAVs. And it is their model which will provide us with usable ideas.

In order to dwell on command and control aspect, it is first essential to remember some important characteristics of UAVs operations. Here the smaller UAVs operated by the Army, like US Army operating 4000 + UAVs are not being considered except for air space management criteria, because these UAVs, being organised at Battalion level have limited area and influence. The discussions are about medium and long endurance UAVs, which give larger ISR picture and also perform many other roles like strike, air to air combat, SEAD, EW, Communication SIG INT & MAS INT etc.

Operationally, UAVs like Predator B, Global Hawk, Heron, Hermes 50 etc. are employed for 24 – 30 hrs plus on each sortie. As we have seen, this duration will gradually increase to 4 – 5 days and then months together. For optimum utilisation they operate at altitudes of 25,000' and above. In future this altitude upper limit will go up to 60000 – 70000 feet. Presently only Global Hawk operates so high. The UAVs have multi sensors, giving them day, night and bad weather capability. Digital architecture would allow real time flow of imagery to whosoever is connected in the network.

The solution to air space management in ongoing operations over Afghanistan and Iraq has been to subdivide the airspace. Airspace up to 3000' above ground level is earmarked for the Army's aviation assets, including the UAVs. Above 3000' airspace is controlled from CAOC in

---

[23] Military Balance, SIPRI 2010. pp. 358 – 362.

[24] Defence News 10 -16 Sep 2001.

order to de-conflict traffic and traffic from other weapons passing through this airspace. All missions above 3000' are tasked through an ATO.[25] Below, 3000' army co-ordinates traffic. There have been reports of collision between army helicopters and UAVs.

We could adopt the same systems. No doubt UAVs are far more economical compared to manned aircraft. But by themselves, these still cost a lot. A package for 8 Herons in 2005 cost US $80 mn. This included the associated ground stations and other equipment.[26] While UAV itself does not have a pilot in the cockpit, a definite advantage in certain circumstances and to the manufacturer, it certainly requires large manpower for operations and maintenance.

A 24 hr sortie, could easily require 4 sets of operating crew. While large portions of the flight profile, including take- off and landing, can be by autopilot, the operators must remain highly vigilant to pick up new ISR inputs and other demands on the UAV. Theoretically, most people could operate and control UAV. The US and the Israeli experience suggests need for active pilots for UAV. This is because regular pilots can have the best situational awareness for optimum employment of UAV. As numbers of UAVs will increase in future, so will their roles and enemy efforts to shoot down UAVs by all possible means. Then the situational awareness will be most critical.[27] USAF has been using F-15 pilots on UAVs. Israelis, by increasingly, the automation in operating, have reduced the UAV crew to two from the initial four.[28]

Realising growing importance and role of UAVs, Israelis have given special attention to UAVs. "There's only one weapon system in Air Force that has its own dedicated HQ level department, and that is the UAVs. So this should indicate how high UAVs are in the realm of priorities."[29]

---

[25] Defence News 13 Feb 2006. p. 44.

[26] Defence News 26 Sep 2006. p. 40.

[27] Defence News 06 Aug 2004. p. 32.

[28] AWST 04 Sep 2000. p. 72.

[29] Defence News 10-16 Sep 2001

5

AIR OPERATIONS CENTRE (AOC)

Command and Controls Imperatives

The fundamental principle in air war has been "centralized planning and decentralized execution". Thus the HQs where centralized planning is done are called Air Operations Centre in the western air forces. In India air wars are planned and executed through various Air Commands, each responsible for certain geographic areas. Today we have five operational commands namely Western Air Command (WAC), South Western Air Command (SWAC), Southern Air Command (SAC), Central Air Command (CAC) and the Eastern Air Command (EAC). Ideally, each front dealing with one hostile power should have only one AOC i.e. only one Command. That's how it was during the WW II at the Burma Front. Post independence, IAF evolved as No. 1 Operational Group, looking after all the units. In 1949, this Operational Group was upgraded to a Command Hq. Then the possibility of a war with China led to creation of No. 1 Operational Group at Calcutta, in 1958. In 1959, this too was upgraded to a Command Hq, namely EAC. Post 1962, Sino-Indian war, CAC was formed at Calcutta, while EAC was moved to Shillong. In 1966, the CAC was moved to Allahabad. WAC then used to look after the entire western border and part of Chinese border in J & K. After the two wars of 1965 and 1971, further reorganisation led to establishment of SWAC in 1980 and SAC in 1984. Such organisations were needed in the poorly connected India- a Sub Continent. Also totally defensive doctrines somewhat made such an arrangement acceptable. Since then revolutionary changes have made the planet a global village and battlefield transparent where targets are found, fixed, tracked and attacked with utmost precision. This demands of us yet another examination of our war fighting organisation. Logic would seem to suggest centralized air operations along western borders at one AOC, along eastern borders at another AOC and towards the south at the third AOC. Also there is the urgent need to create Cyber Command, and Special Operations Command, to meet current and future threats.

Each air command itself needs proper organisation for the inevitable air operations centre for modern warfare. This organisation must be based on following imperatives. The most essential is to build in the FLEXIBILITY in our command and control structures and thought process. While at one extreme, the AOC should fully cater to intense conventional wars, it must be able to simultaneously cater to demands of COIN type operations 24/7 through out the year, year after year. While peace time planning gives ample time to go over various facets of complex air operations, the instant sensor to shooter cycle, superimposed on the few and fleeting targets in COIN operations, necessitates instant response. This was not the requirement when our AOCs in the five operational commands evolved. While intelligence warning of impending conventional war generally gives notice of weeks/ months to prepare and train our manpower for conventional war, the COIN operations require 24/7 response all the time. There is no time to beef up manpower or train untrained personnel. Since political mandate in the modern interconnected world would be imprecise and likely to vary with varying times and circumstances, our AOC and Command structure should have the FLEXIBILITY to adapt to changing goals. This FLEXIBILITY has to permeate our doctrines and training. Our force structure should also cater to inbuilt multi-tasking.

It is essential to have AOC built on mobile, modular and scalable designs. Our SOPs must cater to all possible contingencies of war and COIN operations. This alone will optimise the ever reducing sensor to shooter cycle. Software which is driving all developments evolves after repeated practices and with constantly improving hardware. So we must constantly exercise and practice simulating real time scenarios. Since modern wars are fought through system of systems involving large numbers of personnel, each participant must be encouraged to help systems improvement.

Air Operations Centre (AOC) is established at Command HQ to plan and execute desired air operations. As Air power evolved in the initial years, in the 1930s, it was the Air Defence Command of RAF, which under Air Chief Marshal H Dowding, organised the air defence operations room to control and monitor air defence operations. A proper organisation backed with standardised duties of various functionaries, were established and practiced. In air defence, this was essential as it involved real time control and co-ordination of aircraft observers, aircraft sound detectors, Radars, hoisting of air defence balloons, control of anti – aircraft artillery, scrambling of air defence fighters and their real time coordination against formations of enemy bombers and escort fighters. It was the air defence system of the RAF which saved the day for Britain against Luftwaffe in World War II. It put a stop to the unending run of the so far invincible German war machine.

Air Defence required real time control, whereas Bomber operations did not. And the two operated quite separately. In fact it won't be far from truth to state that Air Defence and Strategic Bombers were two separate Air Forces and operated as such. In current times, AOC has acquired a different character from the AOC, serving the Bomber command in World War II. Now air operations are highly integrated, with all aspects of warfare including land and naval warfare. In modern wars, States try to minimize collateral damage while attacking various targets. Bombing of a city, in order to destroy a target is no more the norm. It was so only during World War II, as a result of very large bombing errors. Now, a plethora of ISR means by way of satellites, aircraft, UAVs etc. produce accurate information on emerging targets that can be quickly located, fixed, tracked and attacked in real time. In a way similar to the air defence operations, a large number of strike operations have become real time and do require adjustments, re-assignment etc. in real time. Thus, a modern AOC includes all facets of air warfare as well as air support of land and naval forces. It also includes information warfare of which cyber war is a major and important component. The modern AOC is quite different from the AOC of the past. One USAF air war planner, describing modern AOC stated, "Streamlined, portable, highly automated CAOC (Combined Air Operations Centre) is more lethal than a ramp full of strike aircraft." The USAF now considers CAOC as a weapon systems called 'Falconer'.

Has our AOC evolved fully on above lines? In order to answer this we need to first study how the modern AOC works and then compare the workings of existing AOC. So what follows is the working of a CAOC in USAF / NATO, these being the unrivalled leaders in air warfare since World War II. It will be highly relevant in our case and more so in the future, because various systems of modern warfare already exist in our midst. All these require extremely fine orchestration and harmonisation. CAOC fulfils this essential requirement.

" Over the last two decades, the military threat to India has changed dramatically toward unconventional war, but the nation's armed forces and national security decision making structure appear not to have made insurgency and terrorism the centre piece of military modernisation effort. "

Stephan P. Cohen[1]

Working of a CAOC

When a war is imminent, the overall commander called C-in-C of the concerned theatre is given objectives from the highest political body. The C-in-C plans his concept of operations (CONOPS) to achieve the stated objectives. The C-in-C then assigns objectives for air war to Air Component Commander who may be Joint Force Air Component Commander (JFACC). We will use the term JFACC in our discussion. The JFACC plans his concept of operations for the air war. Based on this CONOPS, a Master Air Attack Plan (MAAP) is crafted by the air planners' teams. To execute the MAAP, daily mission plans are made and passed to field units for execution via Air Tasking Order (ATO).

An ATO deals with detailed mission planning, force allocation, tasking, Rules of Engagement (ROE) and special considerations, as applicable.

---

[1] Stephan P. Cohen and Sunil Dasgupta," Arming without Aiming: Indian Military Modernisation," Version 16-1. 10 Mar 2010. pp 9-10.

Initially ATO evolved as a three day planning cycle. That meant three teams working on three ATOs simultaneously. These ATOs were for pre-planned targets only. The ATO planners need real time inputs from maintenance, from armament experts, from squadrons and from wings about their operational status and the weather. ATO planners also need combat intelligence inputs.

Combat intelligence was one of the main factors which caused the ATO cycle to be a three day cycle. This was so because during GW- 91, the intelligence set up in USA was more stove–piped than horizontally integrated. The imaging satellites data was provided only at the Continental US (CONUS). The data was centrally processed, to extract intelligence on targets for air tasking. Thereafter, this data was sent to CAOC in Saudi Arabia. This process took time. Similarly inputs from other agencies like NSA, DIA, CIA, etc. also took time. The whole system operated initially on "demand what you want" principle followed by "supply as appropriate from various agencies." Having received diverse inputs from multiple sources, the Intelligence team at CAOC had to collate, process and finally 'Output' the required intelligence. Since then the experience of being continuously at war in Iraq since 1991 and operations in Bosnia in 1995, Kosovo in 1999 and Afghanistan since Oct 2001, the US intelligence system has evolved continuously. The aim has been to provide intelligence output as quickly as possible or real time intelligence against fleeting, mobile targets. The strategy of intelligence system which was a 'Push' system has changed to 'Pull' system, akin to a search on the Google search engine.

The diagram below depicts a simplified version of the Intelligence system, now in vogue:

USA: INTELLIGENCE SYSTEM NETWORK

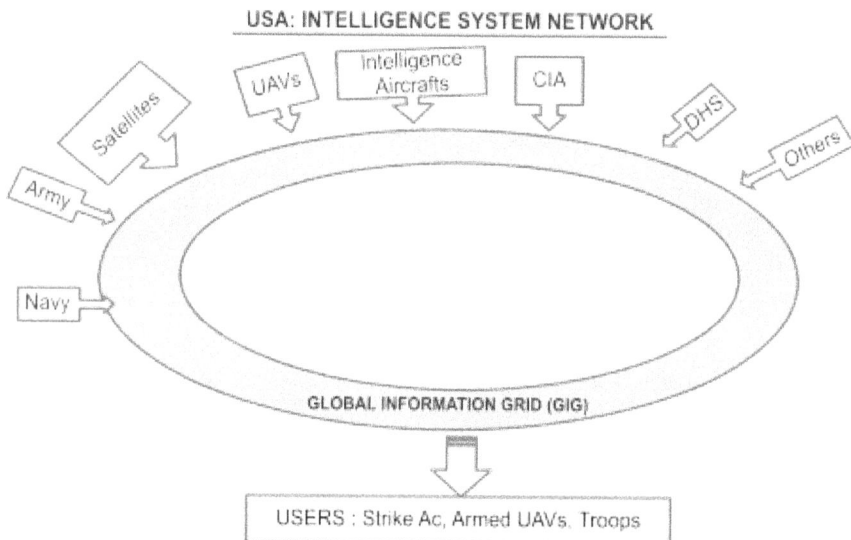

All intelligence systems, command and control centres and weapons are connected to a Global information Grid (GIG). This GIG is a secure network for use for intelligence purposes. The intelligence information is first catalogued and then loaded on to this GIG, even before it has been processed. Thereafter, processing is done. The collection, processing, elimination of duplication etc. is a complex and time consuming process, when done manually. So most of it has been automated to speed up the processing. All services nets are interoperable. A 100 Gb/Sec fibre optic ring is the backbone of this GIG. IP backbone of the system reduces the need to carry servers / communication terminals etc. by each user. Users only need a laptop to plug in. All searches are done by "reach back' to CONUS. The exact nomenclature for intelligence grid is "Distributed Common Ground System" (DGCS) and it has continued to evolve.[2] The DGCS is served by a Network controller – which is the brain and the central nervous system. The central computer, common protocols, language and

[2] Defence News 08 Mar 04

54

algorithms, the platform interface module, working in synchronisation, improve the target location accuracy to 20 feet. The system was capable of detecting 1000 targets per hour in 2002.[3]

An individual needing intelligence inputs, plugs into the GIG, like we log on to Google on the internet. Then he searches for information on desired targets. The search engine loaded on GIG, gives a Google like fast response, showing links to the desired information. The user selects the desired link to obtain the required information. This is how this 'Pull' system of intelligence works. Basically it avoids the overloads which invariably result in a "push" system. It is fast and delivers intelligence after processing inputs of multiple agencies. The users too are connected on a high band width net – so video streaming, including live occurrences is easily possible.

The fact that all agencies are connected on this global highway means each agency can operate from its parent location wherever it may be. They do not have to move to the area of operation with all associated infrastructure. The user deploys for operations with only front – end devices and plugs into the GIG. The back end and heavy stuff remains at its permanent location, often in CONUS. This not only avoids the hassle of moving bag and baggage of many units, it keeps the units safe from hostile fire, at home location and permits most optimum operation. GIG being global, the system works equally well anywhere on the globe. The automation in the GIG processing also confers another major advantage. It avoids overlap in multiple sensors viewing field in real time. The various sensors starting from imaging satellites to UAVs close to ground have varying resolution and imaging capability. The automation process also selects correct sensors for different tasks and slews them in real time, as required.[4]

The change to horizontal ISR from vertical ISR is best explained by Lieutenant General Deve Deptula, a leading thinker in USAF. "...we will move from our historical industrial age, military culture that far too long has segregated operations from intelligence, to a culture better suited to the

---

[3] AW & ST, 11 Nov 2002, p. 23.

[4] Defence News 31 Oct 05

information age one that integrates operations and intelligence, producing unprecedented synergies in action, accuracy and effectiveness."[5] He argues that earlier ISR operations were like a farmer's operations of sowing, growing, harvesting and supplying ISR intelligence to Operations. This cyclic process was not useful against time critical targets, like mobile scuds and elusive and fleeting small targets of war on terror. Therefore, the ISR must be Hunter ISR. ISR in real time should be fully integrated horizontally between all sensors. It should be intimately connected with operations. This would require new doctrine, tactics, architecture and integration.

While the above argument is sound, the actual implementation would have to be tempered with practical lessons during trials, exercises and operations. Excessive technology should not lead to information overload and little intelligence. An observer noted, "There is a ground swell of opinion that suggests that solution lies in FMV (Full Motion Video). Receive Only Video Enhanced Receiver (ROVER) is in use with several ground units in Iraq giving the Predator FMV picture to local commanders. Despite the attraction of 24/7 video, the spell – binding download from Predator and other UAVs, it is fairly limited in value. As with a still image, unless interpreted by an image analyst, it is often hard to discern the relevance of what one sees. Colour, high – resolution video gives plenty of information but little intelligence because it cannot show intent."[6]

The horizontal integration of all ISR sensors with command and control centres and weapons is not a luxury. It is an essential requirement in modern warfare. Unlike the past wherein kinetic attacks by strike aircraft were the only offensive means, now a variety of means for offence, exist. These are cyber attacks, electronic warfare attacks, non-lethal attacks, high power microwave attacks, psychological deception operations etc. All these could be used either singly, or in combination. More often than not, it is the coordinated manner which is the most preferred option. To do so mandates

---

[5] Lt Gen(Retd) Deve Deptula, Col Mike Francisco USAF, " Air Force ISR Operations," Air & Space Power Journal. 2010 Fall

[6] Gp Capt RM Poole, "The Utility of Air Power in Nation Building," The RAF Air Power Review Summer 2005, p. 171.

horizontal integration for finding the best attack opportunity, executing the attack and monitoring the effectiveness of orchestrated attack.

As and when the strikes, based on ATO, are undertaken, the operations staff in CAOC monitors the ATO execution. ATO is a plan based on a variety of factors. These factors do change from the assumed ones after creating the ATO. Therefore, in real time, adjustments will have to be made. This is another important function of operations staff at CAOC. The adjustments could be concerning types of strike aircraft, their numbers, the weapon carried, new or different targets, unexpected enemy opposition, weather, air refuelling, AWACS support and so on.

The nature of air war is different from that of naval or land warfare. Initially the Air Force is fully engaged in battle of air – superiority and ongoing parallel interdiction campaign. But as the air superiority is attained and it leads to command of air, plenty of combat aircrafts are released for other tasks namely greater support of land and naval battle. Also with the introduction of smaller precision weapons, due to far superior explosives in the war head – it is possible to carry larger numbers of weapons on each strike aircraft. It is akin to significantly increasing the size of available air power. In 2003, a B-2 bomber could carry 84 JDAMs, each capable of destroying one target. This was to increase to 200 JDAMS in future. A fighter aircraft can carry 15 – 20 such bombs in one sortie, with each bomb capable of destroying one target. So equipped, an Air Force can engage many targets simultaneously in each mission. A dynamic ISR system can detect emerging targets and gainfully employ the abundant strike power. Thus, the CAOC not only caters to pre – planned air tasking, but also includes real time air tasking against new emerging targets. The targets could be enemy army pitted against our army, enemy reinforcements and supplies, mobile rocket launchers or even few fleeting targets in insurgency warfare.

A phenomenal amount of automation has been built into CAOC, working to reduce the manpower as well as to make it more responsive for tackling emerging targets. During Gulf War 91, a CAOC was manned by 750 personnel. By Aug 2002, it had been down sized to 250 with further reductions aimed at 100-125 personnel. Similarly the three day ATO cycle was reduced to 101 minutes by KOSOVO 1999 conflict. It was further reduced to 19 minutes in Afghanistan, post 2001. But these were special cases and do not represent routine ATO cycles.

The above improvements have been possible due to a number of steps. Some of these are mentioned below. CAOC has been declared an operational unit called 'Falconer." So it must work like any other operational unit. It has dedicated trained manpower. Presently USA has eight CAOCs. Of these, three are functional CAOCs located in CONUS. Two CAOCs are tailorable for Global strike and special operations. One CAOC is a training unit while another CAOC is an experimental unit, used to constantly evolve the CAOC and its functioning.

Like other operational units, 'Falconer' or AN/USQ – 163 gets its "initial operational capability" by Commanders in Chief. Subsequently it achieves 'Full operational capability'. The CAOC runs dummy exercises to train the staff. A massive modelling and simulation centre, located in Florida, simulates and feeds all air exercises including downed aircrafts and insurgent activity.

An exercise designed for CAOC training, called 'Blue Flag' teaches strategy, planning procedures, targeting, execution and process to employ air, space and information operations in a major Theatre campaign. In order to trigger exercise participants, battlefield tactics, techniques and procedures, the entire CAOC is brought up to wartime manning. This is a seven day exercise which has three days of academic training and four days of exercise. Training of senior officers is at operational level. Retired Generals are employed for mentoring. Since 2005, CAOC is integrated in USAF's Red Flag exercise to train CAOC personnel under most realistic operational conditions.

Electronic Systems Centre (ESC) of the USAF constantly designs, modifies and upgrades the software used in CAOC and other specialist aircrafts like the AWACS, Rivet Joint, Compass Call etc. The ESC sets up the PCs/ monitors and the software in CAOC and keeps updating them periodically. The ESC designs various systems in the CAOC and decides on required hardware and software. They are, in effect, System Managers.

ESC works with the industry in getting the system made and its procurement. During CAOC exercises, ESC injects new equipment and software for testing. This way they also get feedback and ideas for further improvements. They support the CAOC during operations, providing solution to various issues as they crop up. A major improvement in CAOC connectivity was achieved during JFEX 2007. AWACS was connected to CAOC using a high bandwidth Internet Protocol – enabled radio, specialised software applications and an air – borne web-server. The system connected the AWACS to the CAOC and similarly – equipped platforms to perform command & control and battle management functioning, using machine to machine technology over an airborne network. This is called Tactical Targeting Network Technology (TTNT). The TTNT capability allowed multiple platforms to digitally share command and control information, more than ever before, providing common situation awareness across the entire kill chain. The AWACS equipped with a TTNT, used an internet connection to successfully obtain real time Blue Force tracking data, Air Tasking orders and ATO updates and weather information. AWACS was able to publish its air picture at the sensor level to the ground in real time for the first time. Aircrew's situational awareness was also greatly expanded by adding the ground picture. Thus, time sensitive targets were no longer a surprise to the AWACS crew. Instead, through the use of chat and various other applications, with a connection directly to the CAOC, the crews could watch and anticipate the development of Time Sensitive Targets. AWACS crews were able to develop synergetic relationships with CAOC and move strike aircraft into position early or adjust fuelling time in anticipation of dynamic tasking. Other aircraft equipped with TTNT include E – 8, RC – 135 V/W Rivet Joint, B1 and B2.

Another way to reduce manpower and optimise CAOC was introduction of 'Trusted thin Client'. This created more working space because of one central server. It allowed many networks, even with different security classifications to be viewed on one screen, thereby reducing the number of PCs and manpower. Even while reducing manpower on one side, a new additional task of Theatre Missile Defence has been added in CAOC.

The software used for generating ATO is called Theatre Battle management core system. It is a web enabled system, providing better information flow into CAOC. The system is scalable and modular, across the spectrum of conflict and readily able to accept innovation. The ISR software is called "ISR Manager". It displays location of all ISR sensors and their fields of look. It helps dynamic re-tasking of sensors. The MAAP tool kit, another software, has reduced ATO making time by 85 percent and work stations tenfold.

The CAOC basically has five divisions. First is the Strategy Division. It comprises four teams, dealing with Strategy Plans, Strategy Guidance, Operational Assessment and Information Operation team. The next division is Combat Plans Division. These too comprise of four teams, dealing with Target Effects team, MAAP team, ATO production team and Command and Control Planning team. The third division is Combat Operations Division. This comprises six teams, namely Offensive Operations team, Defensive Operations team, Personal Recovery, Senior Intelligence Duty Officer, Interface Control and Weather Specialty team. The fourth division is ISR Division. This deals with Analysis, co-relation, fusion; targeting and tactical assessment and ISR operations. The fifth is the Air Mobility Division. It includes Commanders Support Staff, Air Mobility Control team, Air lift Control team, Air Refuelling team and Aero Medical Evacuation Control team.

In 2006, a Battlefield co-ordination detachment was inducted into CAOC. At the same time, an Air Operation Centre detachment was located with the Army. This resulted in better integration, small and reduced ATO cycles, reduced to 44 hours from 72 hours, for counter insurgency operations.

In addition, each CAOC has attachable modules, dealing with cyber war, electronic warfare, information operation, with respect to hostile TV network, Radio network, telephone exchanges etc. The other modules deal with space support, non kinetic weapons, mobile scud type targets.[7]

Commenting on lessons from Afghanistan war, Benjamin S. Lambeth stated, "...the dominance of fused information over platforms and munitions

---

[7] AWST 23 Sep 02. p. 21.

was the principle enabler of campaign success".[8] The evolution of CAOC, has seen competing demands on it. On one hand is the need for standardisation so that proper training is given; standards are laid down and implemented in designing and procurement. The support staff and the cadre training is streamlined. On the other hand, customisation and modernisation put differing demands. Customisation results in designing user specific systems, location specific and mission specific systems. Modernisation is required in acquiring latest hardware and evolving software. Thus, while following the standard concept, the individual CAOCs do differ in certain aspects dealing with data presentation. Described below is organisation in a CAOC.

In a large enclosure housing four or more large screens of 10 feet x 10 feet, 75 personnel sit in three semi – circular rows. Screen one on the left, shows location and identity of all ground and airborne weapons and sensor systems. Approximate range rings around weapon system shows its coverage area. Here the 'Finders' locate targets and track them. Confirmed targets are handed over to 'Deciders'.

---

[8] Benjamin S. Lambeth, " Air power Against Terror - Americans' Conduct of Operation Enduring Freedom," RAND 2006. p. 30

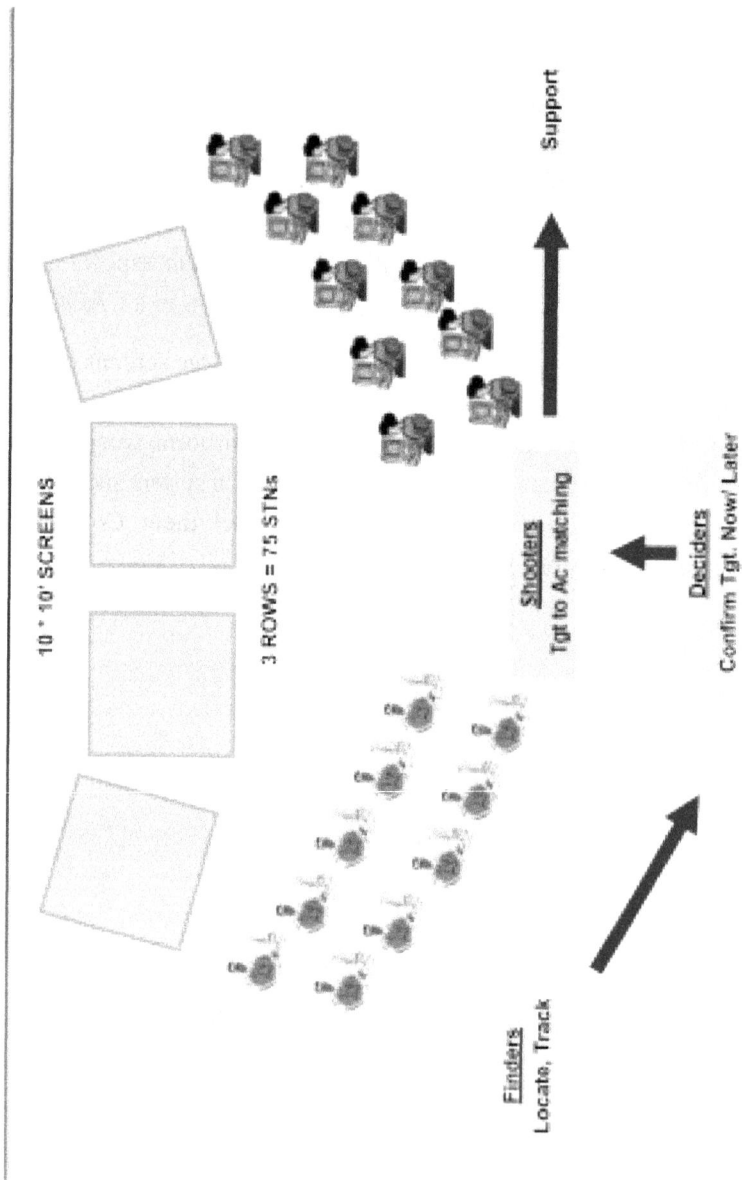

Combined Air Operations Centre

10' * 10' SCREENS

3 ROWS = 75 STNs

Finders
Locate, Track

Shooters
Tgt to Ac matching

Deciders
Confirm Tgt. Now/ Later

Support

Screen two shows the dynamic target list. The Deciders prioritise the targets, select suitable weapon options for each target and hand these over to the 'Shooter'. Screen three is the air situation board. It shows the location of friendly and enemy aircrafts. It gets its input from radars and AWACS. Screen four shows the common operational picture. Common operational picture shows location of and identity of Air, Land and Naval Forces. This picture is used by Deciders to build up battle space awareness.

US Experience: CAOC

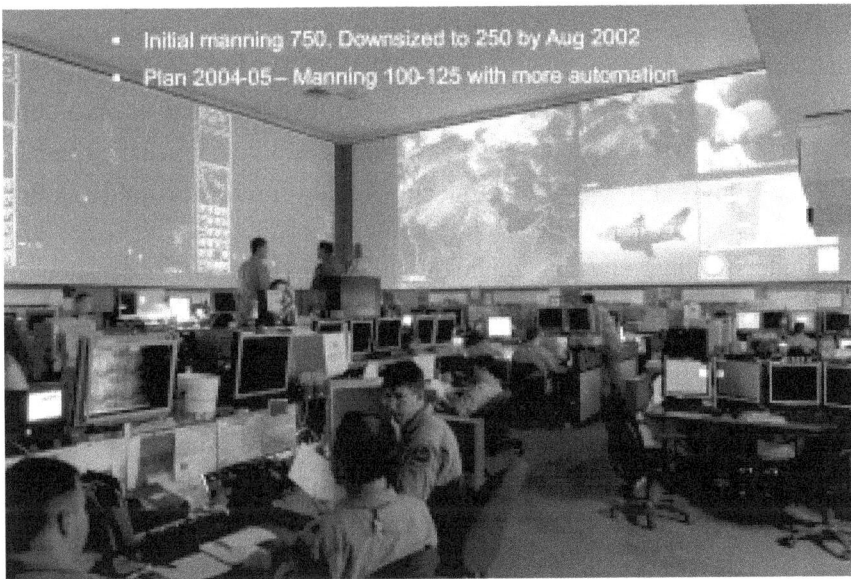

In addition, other options for screen display are weather pictures, TV news flashes, graphic display of imagery satellites showing their location and coverage area, etc. These are displayed as and when asked by Chief of Operations. CAOC is also connected to the mobile trailers, housing Cyber War Cell, EW Cell, Space Control Cell, Information Operations Cell, to control hostile TV station, Radio Station, telephone exchanges, mobile scud type launchers command and control cabin and non-kinetic weapons cell. Any or all of these operations are undertaken with proper synchronisation with rest of the operations.

Deciders confirm the correct target and decide if the target is to be engaged immediately or at a later time. Then they pass the data to the Shooters. The Shooters have data on available weapon systems. They match the targets with the best weapon system and pass the necessary ATO. In addition, the shooters co-ordinate with support staff for requirements of air refuelling, AWACS cover etc.

The communication within the CAOC and with associated cells is mostly on Text Chat Rooms. Various Text Chat Rooms dealing with each item/ subject are created. These could include time critical targeting, Intelligence, UAV, refuelling, space etc. Also communication with crew manning stations onboard AWACS, Rivet Joint, Compass Call, JSTARS etc and CAOC staff is also on Text Chat Room. The chat room text is displayed on a large screen for everyone's situational awareness. In addition, voice interphones also provide communication, but are not the preferred mode. Voice communication – experience has shown- produces more errors and misunderstanding. The diagram below shows control of UAV operations in real time at an AOC. It is important to note that the text chat is displayed on the top right corner for everyone's information. The various agencies, some located far apart, are chatting in real time, using text chat.

UAV Real Time

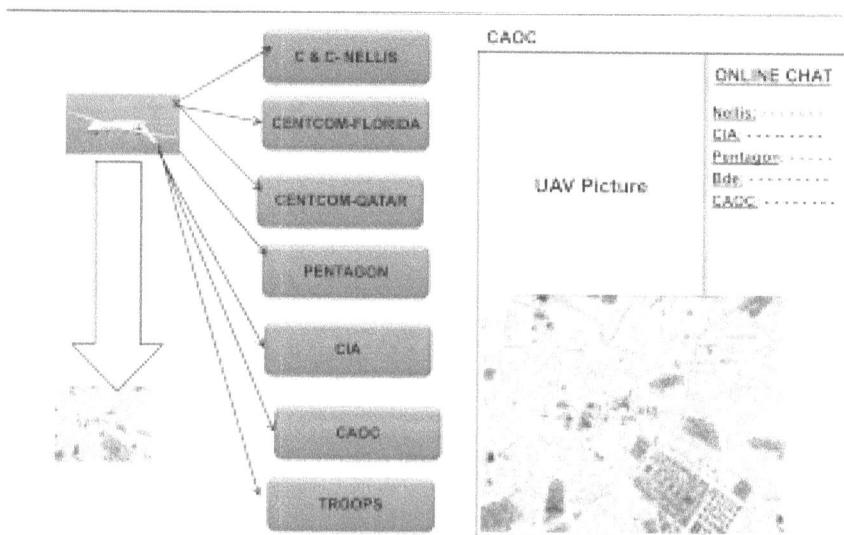

64

Having studied the US model, we could undertake the following, to refine our AOC:

1. Visit CAOCs in USAF, RAF, NATO and Israel.

2. Co-opt software industry from the word go.

3. Initially develop one model for evolution.

4. Make a Core Team from start to finish.

5. Develop ROE for all contingencies and practice them regularly to refine them.

6. All intelligence agencies must be networked for a "pull" system to extract intelligence information.

7. Intelligence information sharing must be on a Google like search architecture.

8. Automate intelligence fusion and processing, continuously.

9. Command exercises must include Cyber Ops integration in real time.

10. EW & Cyber Ops Dtes should be built on a modular model at Air Hq. They should have multiple teams to be attached to needed Command, on an as required basis.

11. Explore non-lethal weapons.

12. Create dedicated cadre of Intelligence officers at par with operations.

13. Create AOC at WAC, EAC, SAC and one for training. Post dedicated manpower to operate them 24/7.

6

COUNTER SURFACE FORCE OPERATIONS (CSFO)

" In contrast to strategic bombing, air support for armies was determined by levels of developed doctrine and training rather than prevailing levels of technology. The Luftwaffe had few, if any, high quality close air support aircraft, yet by 1939 it was a potent ground attack force, owing to it's carefully honed doctrine. In contrast, the US air force had many new and technologically advanced aircrafts, but lacked the doctrine to apply them successfully."

John Buckly in "Air Power in the Age of Total War"

Problems of CSFO

Victory has many fathers- failure is an orphan. In the euphoria of victory, the problems that were encountered in the conduct of war, are either forgotten or find an insignificant mention. Whereas a variety of reasons are easily identified, which led to failure. Command and control failure generally finds a central place.

The lightning victory of MNF over Iraq during GW–1991 seemed to suggest the perfect integration and jointmanship amongst MNF, especially between the Air Forces and the Armies in the Theatre. In reality, this was not so flawless as it seemed. There were problems. Gen Tommy Franks, Commander VII Corps, the heavy mechanised formation responsible for direct attack, northwards into Iraq, was less than satisfied with the air support he received, prior to the commencement of war, as well as during the dynamic four days of ground war. The problems – as perceived by the land commanders - were a result of doctrinal differences and the actual procedure adopted for the Gulf War.

Doctrine being a core statement of the ways of war fighting, is purposely kept brief, as long as the key principles of warfare are clearly enunciated. In reality, actual wars are characterised by different circumstances and innumerable other associated factors. This then requires intelligent adaptation of doctrinal principles to the existing situation. The varying perceptions of different commanders to these adaptations, is what causes friction.

The next point is about technological advancements. These impact warfare and alter its conduct as the reach, intensity and precision of fire power improves. Doctrines are seldom changed at the same pace of technological changes, to incorporate latest advancements in application of fire power. This too, causes friction between the Army and Air Force.

There is another point, creating immense confusion is the nature of war- whether static or dynamic. Let us, for ease of understanding, imagine a front line of 1000 km across whish hostile armies are deployed. The land commanders on each side are trying to select two to three attack avenues. Their aim is to find a suitable avenue of attack; to be able to breach the forward defences quickly and launch the major manoeuvre force to encircle the hostile army. So, in effect, this 1000 km front is quite alive but with rather low intensity fire fight, both prior to and during the actual attack, except at places where armies are trying to create a breach for an eventual break through. The diagram below aims to present this situation wherein the rectangles represent the areas of likely, intense fighting.

So, to the various land commanders on this front, the frontline could be non-active, less active and highly active depending upon the intensity of fighting. Now let us visualise as to how an air commander views this frontage. The 1000 km front, which could easily have around 4-6 Corps HQs, would have only one air commander, responsible for air operations, because the combat aircraft can easily cover this entire frontage, in a matter of an hour or so and engage targets, wherever demanded.

It is presumed that the reader is well versed with the nuances of Counter Surface Force Operations (CSFO) and knows the difference between air interdiction(AI), battle field air interdiction(BAI) and battle field airstrike (BAS). To refresh, AI is executed against targets, which were planned jointly by the Air Force and Army, but which do not require any coordination for execution in real time. BAI targets, similarly planned, are attacked when the Army wants. However, its execution does not require real time co-ordination. The BAS requires close co-ordination with fire and movement of the Army. All this was good in the World War II. With the advent of long range artillery, rockets and missiles and attack helicopters, new problems of coordination between air strikes and organic weapons cropped up. The GW-91, which saw incorporation of long range weapons with land forces, threw up co-ordination problems during the war. Our own prevailing situation is quite similar and likely to pose similar problems. So it is proposed to study the command and control problems of GW-91.

During the 38 day air campaign, barring the battle of Al-Khafji, wherein two Iraqi divisions, launched an attack on Saudi Arabia and were decimated quickly, there was no ground fighting. The air campaign could be executed, following only one set of CONOPS. In fact some innovative concepts were also tried out which may find a place in some of our future operations. The Air Forces were clear to strike targets, north of Iraqi border defences. The targets were jointly planned at CENTCOM HQ. There was little co-ordination required with the fielded ground forces. The area north of the Iraqi border was divided into kill boxes each measuring 32x32 kms. Generally, the land commanders kept these kill boxes open for air attacks. If they did not wish air strikes in any particular kill box, they could declare that kill box closed. A fast airborne FAC, flying a fighter jet, controlled strikes in the kill box. The attacking aircraft adopted medium level attack profiles, to keep safe from intense anti aircraft artillery.

When the dynamic ground war commenced, the requirement of close air support (BAS) also commenced. This necessitated close and detailed integration with the surface fire and movement plan. Let us see the organic fire power that was available with the VII Corps and the XVIII airborne Corps. The VIII Corps had attack helicopters, utility helicopters, the ATCAMS (Advance Tactical Missiles) and the long range artillery. Their range was from 100 km to 150 km plus. Their utilisation was with the Corp HQ. In this airspace, if BAS from air force fighters was needed-then perforce detailed integration was required. That is to silence the surface weapons in the airspace in which air force/navy jets would operate to provide BAS. It is not a good option in the midst of a dynamic war. That too when the Iraqis were retreating rapidly and the MNF, advancing at a furious pace.

The Americans demarcate the battle area needing detailed integration by FSCL (Fire Support Coordination Line). Most other Air Forces call it the Bomb line. It is a line based on ground features, terrain permitting and hopefully is easily recognisable by the pilot, in a fast moving jet, while simultaneously looking for ground targets and hostile fighters. Beyond the FSCL, BAI is permitted. Within FSCL, only BAS can be undertaken. If one has a FSCL well, deep into enemy area in order to give more freedom to the organic fire power, one is in effect reducing amount of possible BAS. In GW-91, plenty of BAS was available but remained under-utilised.

The fighters normally operate at a speed of 15 km/minute or a km every four seconds. Their turn radius is in several kilometres. This makes their area of manoeuvre, quite large. So perforce a large area has to be kept free of organic weapons activity. While BAS is needed only at one or two specific points, in order to allow fighters to operate safely over a large area, organic weapons have to be kept silent over this entire area, needed for the fighters to manoeuvre. The diagram below illustrates this.

GROUND WAR

BAI Area

FSCL

Silence Zone – Organic Fire Power

BAS Area

XX

ENEMY SIDE

BAS Area

FRONT LINE

OWN SIDE

XX

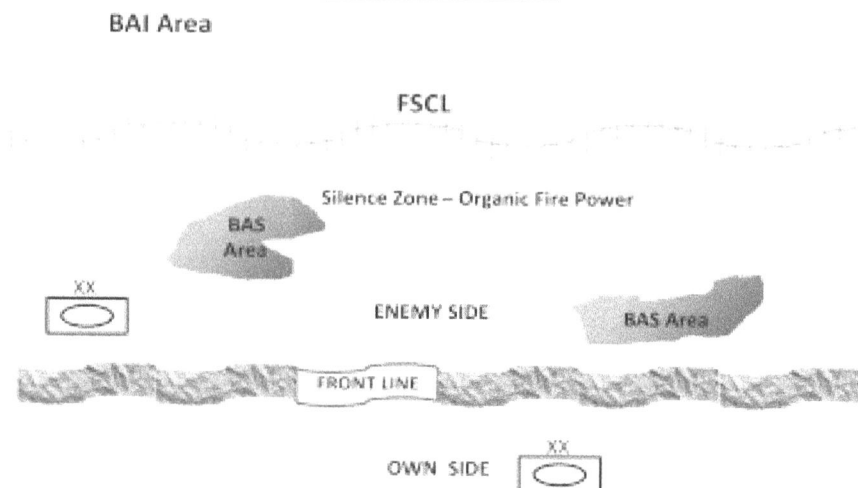

With XVIII airborne Corps, the situation worsened even more. Being airborne corps, they launched a heli-borne attack. Coming from lesser contested directions, their advance was extremely rapid. This pushed their ideal FSCL even deeper. But in the adjacent VIII Corps, fighting remained further back. See simplified diagram below.

MNF GROUND ATTACK : GULF WAR – 91

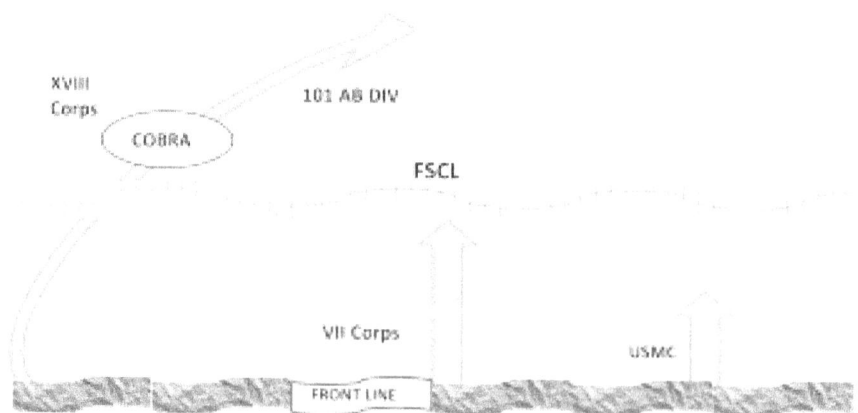

XVIII Corps

101 AB DIV

COBRA

FSCL

VII Corps

USMC

FRONT LINE

While this FSCL was fine for VII Corps, it was not ideal for XVIII Corps. So, while plenty of BAS was available, it could not be used in 101 airborne division area because they were 80 nm north of designated FSCL. It is not that the commanders did not realise these problems. But by the time solutions were devised, precious time was lost and many Iraqi Republican Guards escaped destruction from MNF air power.

The kill boxes in KTO (Kuwaiti Theatre of Operation) were generally kept closed. These kill boxes were opened only when air strikes were directed into them. This arrangement was because of closer proximity of MNF ground forces to the kill boxes.

Inside FSCL, no weapon could be released unless cleared by an FAC. ABCCC (Airborne Command Control Centre on C – 130 Hercules) and AWACS regularly updated aircrew on FSCL and position of ground troops in KTO. A fast FAC (F – 16) or killer scout was required to control the BAI mission within 54 kms from FSCL, towards the enemy side to act as a buffer, between BAI & BAS.

To get more freedom for organic ATACMS, MLRS, and Attack Helicopters the land commander wanted to move FSCL forward by 100 – 150 km. The commander of XVIII airborne corps, advancing even faster with heliborne attack wanted it even further out to allow more freedom to army helicopters. The GWAPS (Gulf War Air power Survey) summary report states that moving the FSCL out, "was to hamper airpower's ability to destroy escaping Iraqi ground forces until the FSCL was finally pulled back. GWAPS Vol II, Operations, expands the story," By moving the line (FSCL) forward, the (XVIII) airborne corps staff avoided having to put their helicopters under Air Force Control. That decision, however, had unforeseen consequences; XVIII airborne corps had created a situation that severely limited the potential of coalitions' available firepower. Despite the fact that no US ground troops were north of the Euphrates – nor were there plans for such a movement – Navy and Air Force aircrafts now could only attack the causeway and high way, north of the Euphrates under direct control of FACs. But virtually all the FACs were concentrated in supporting troops in combat, south in Kuwait. Moreover, conditions were not favorable for the employment of FACs even if they had been available… In the end, the TAC (Tactical Air Control Centre) appealed to Schwarz Kopf to move the FSCL back to the Euphrates, so that air strikes could hit both the causeway and the roads, north of the river."[1]

Co-location of Commanders

Co-location of both Army and Air Hq, along with respective commanders was the foremost lesson, emerging from past wars. Today Hqs and subordinate organisations are highly networked, both horizontally as well as vertically. This may, rightfully, create an impression that while being physically well apart, networking results in instant sharing of information and thus overcomes the need to physically co-locate the commanders. Nothing would be further from the truth. It is most important for the commanders to interact face to face, as much as possible. This alone eliminates the misperception, friction etc and gives rise to a true joint plan. Whereas the staff may be physically located at different places, the problems are less, because the staff gets correct directions from their co-located commanders. Failure to do so i.e., CENTCOM HQ being at Tampa, Florida, US and Air Component Commander, being at CAOC in Saudi Arabia during Op Enduring Freedom (Afghanistan war) did cause quite a lot of friction and some poor Joint Planning.[2]

Sensor to Shooter Time Cycle & Targeting Approval Process

Today's ISR capabilities, and more so in future, by highly persistent platforms and better sensors, coupled with integrated intelligence analysis algorithms will provide large number of real time / near real time targets. As an example the mission planning time to use Tomahawk cruise missile during Gulf War – 91, was three days. It reduced to 101 minutes during Kosovo War of 1999. US still reduced it further to 19 min during 2001 war in Afghanistan. By nature these targets would be fleeting targets, mostly human beings in

---

[1] Major Terrance J. Mccaffrey III, " What Happened to BAI? Army and Air Force Battlefield Doctrine Development From Pre Desert Storm To 2001," School of Advanced Air Power Studies, Air University, Alabama USA, 2002. p. 57.

[2] Lambeth, Ibid, p.XXV

small numbers. To target them, instant decision to engage them would be an essential requirement. This brings to the fore, some relevant questions. Who would be the deciding authority to permit target engagement? How high up in the hierarchical chain would the authority rest? Will the SOP, drawn up for a full fledged war, wherein certain amount of mistakes leading to collateral damage may be acceptable, still apply in peacetime situations, dealing with terrorists/insurgents amongst our innocent population? Can this SOP be flexibly tailored for differing situations? Will it be rigid in adapting to different prevailing situations? There are no easy answers. Yet absence of answers, howsoever imperfect, would be worse than no answer at all and it will negate the advantages provided by the technology.

War after war, nations continue to learn and relearn the same lessons. For e.g. the USA's prosecution of war in Vietnam from 1965 – 72 was beset with the problem of target selection and clearance at the President's level. US improved upon this decision making process, during Gulf War of 1991. Yet again during the war in Afghanistan in 2001, US was beset with the lengthy process of target verification and authorisation at CENTCOM level. Despite excellent networking, this often delayed the sensor to shooter cycle; at other times it dictated engagement of less suitable targets by air power, mainly because the land & air commanders were located geographically, eight time zones apart.[3]

Flexibility and Innovation in BAS

Present system of demanding BAS is not clear on what the desired effects on the target, are. Generally, in an intense conventional war, the desired effect is destruction of the target, most of the time. But even in conventional operations and more so in operations dealing with insurgents / anti national elements, if the 'effect' desired on the target is mentioned, the BAS would become more immediate and effective. Giving elaboration on this point to the US House of Representatives Armed Services Committee, Lt Gen Buchanass stated, "On December 29, 2003, Forward Operating Base St

---

[3] Lambeth, Ibid, p.XXII

Mere came under mortar attack. The 3rd BCT Fire Support element counter – battery radar fixed the point of origin and within 20 seconds, the point of origin was passed from the air liaison officer to the MQ-1 (Predator) crew. Eighty – five seconds after the attack, the MQ-1 had located and was tracking two vehicles, fleeing the point of origin, at a high rate of speed. The MQ-1 was directed to follow the southern most vehicle, as a quick response force was assembled. Forty – five minutes into the engagement, the quick response force from the 82nd Air Borne apprehended the subject that were tracked by MQ-1".

Probably this was so due to ROE. However, if effect desired was destruction, then the MQ-1 could have destroyed the vehicle within a minute, by onboard weapons. And both vehicles could have been attacked. In future, as non lethal weapons come into regular usage, "effect" desired could be calibrated into the weapons (HPM, Laser) itself. A small point though important enough, especially in insurgency operations.[4]

Here is yet another example of novel use of the ISR data. The data architecture has been so built that the video of the sensor, fitted on the BAS fighter aircraft, is being passed on to the Air Liaison Officer (ALO), controlling the mission. So the ALO, by seeing the video, can control the aircraft by ultimate talk on – "left a bit, right a bit – that is the target". Indeed a novel mix of technology and operating procedure.[5]

Then again, distinct from traditional conventional war, we may be engaged in expeditionary type of operations – say for example in our Island territories, or two fronts being active, simultaneously and need to relocate forces from one front to another, in order to meet developing, adverse eventualities. In such cases, the amount of BAS contribution and it's impact could be far more, compared to organic fire power. This trend has been observed in Iraq in 2002. "...In contemporary warfare, the success of air power in providing day, night, adverse – weather, precision air support for ground forces etc. has convinced the Army leadership that it can make its

---

[4] Ibid RM Poole. p. 19.

[5] Ibid Poole. p. 19

forces more deployable and agile by reducing its own organic fire support, such as artillery, and relying more heavily on air power." This was reflected in Iraq, in 2003. Of the 19898 targets struck, over 15000 were through BAS missions.[6] Of course, this was in a totally asymmetric air situation. In our case, the demands of two front war will so stretch the resources, that there will be little air effort available, unless of course, we structure the Air Force properly. The present notion of a 45 Squadron Air Force, as a sufficient force for war, does not satisfy the mathematical logic and requires thorough reexamination. But in other situations, where we have asymmetrical advantage, the above proposition makes sense.The Kargil conflict in 1999 was one such case, where we made excellent use of air asymmetry in our favour. Counter Insurgency operations and policing operations again give us the asymmetrical advantage. Imaginative employment of Air power can help us deal with these situations, with lesser foot prints on the ground.

Kill Boxes

Traditionally, BAS is sub divided between immediate and pre-planned. Immediate BAS is mostly fire fighting to correct an adverse situation. Pre-planned BAS is the result of proper planning and prior intelligence. Being less restrictive in execution, it is easier to plan. Preponderance of Air power allows one more category of BAS. It was called 'Cab Rank' in World War II. Now the US calls it 'Push CAS'. It means one has surplus aircrafts, air borne, awaiting targets to emerge. As the targets pop up, these waiting aircraft are pushed forward. Similar was the case in 1971 Indo – Pak war in the eastern sector. IAF, having secured the skies in the first 48 hours, could push all available efforts into Push BAS and Interdiction. The latter was purposely kept low as pure destruction was not the primary aim.

The concept of kill boxes is one step further in BAS to enlarge the scope of BAI. This started in the Gulf War 91 and has been used thereafter in Afghanistan and Iraq, to good effect. The enemy surface area is divided into squares measuring 32 km X 32 km. These are further sub divided,

---

[6] Wg Cdr Harv Smyth, "Air Power Review" Spring 2007 – 'From Coningham to Project Coningham – Keyes." p. 1.

sometimes into four squares, sometimes nine squares or more as shown below:

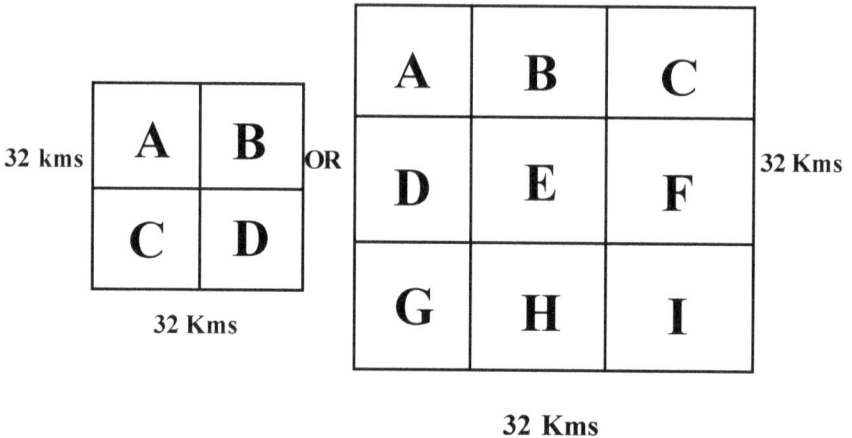

A	B	C
D	E	F
G	H	I

32 kms

A	B
C	D

OR

32 Kms

32 Kms

32 Kms

The kill boxes were marked on the map and passed on to all the agencies. The kill boxes which were between FLOT and FSCL were under the control of local ground commanders. Kill boxes beyond FSCL were controlled by JFACC. If the ground commander wanted air interdiction in kill boxes under his jurisdiction, he would declare the kill box open and CAOC would then assign air effort to it. The opening and closing of the kill box could vary in duration, depending upon time. This indeed was a neat solution, to co-ordinate ground and air fire in a zone. It also simplified air space co-ordination between Air Force aircraft, Army aircraft, UAVs, and organic fire consisting of ATCAMS, MLRS, Artillery etc.

The method of working a kill box during Gulf War- 91 was something like this. A pair of aircraft, mostly F – 16, would be assigned a few kill boxes. While one F – 16 maintained top cover, another F – 16 would descend to lower levels, maintaining high speed, to search for targets. Once the target was spotted, BAS aircraft would be called in. The BAS aircraft would pick up the target from safe height, using their sensors and drop precision weapons. Only A – 10s, with armour protection against 23 mm, were permitted to attack from low levels. Their 30 mm Galling Gun and above wing mounted twin engines, helped BAS from low levels while keeping attrition within acceptable limits. Having attained air superiority and being in no hurry to start a ground war – which Saddam Hussein desperately wanted - MNF cleverly utilised available sorties to work enemy forces, proceeding systematically via the kill box route. By the 38th day of war, which was only the air war so far, MNF claimed destruction of 1745 tanks, 1549 artillery pieces and 945 ICVs.

The desert terrain and available technology combination was brilliantly exploited by the Americans. The Iraqis would bury their tanks in the sand, making it invisible to a naked eye. But the IR sensors could easily pick up the buried tanks due to heat contrast and were thus targeted with LGBs. Hundreds of buried tanks were destroyed this way. During the preceding war with Iran, Iraqi soldiers felt most safe, when safely inside their tanks. During the Gulf War- 91 and thereafter, the inside of the tank became the most unsafe place for a soldier. This shows the impact of precision Air attacks on the modern battlefield. The same pattern was followed in Afghanistan, during Op Enduring Freedom in 2001 and thereafter. Afghanistan battlefield was not so clearly divided as in Gulf War – 91. The non – linear nature of frontline was applicable here in which friendly forces were spread far apart. Such a battlefield has lesser pre-planned targets versus emerging targets, needing immediate BAS. This was borne out by facts. Benjamin S. Lambeth, an air power analyst observed, "... Although these engagement zones were similar to kill boxes that had been set up during Operation Desert Storm a decade earlier, they did not allow allied aircrew to attack anything that moved inside them without prior CENTCOM approval because persistent uncertainties, regarding the location of friendly Afghan opposition forces and allied Special Operation Forces (SOF) in close proximity to known or suspected enemy positions. Nevertheless, their establishment did indicate an impending move away from pre-planned targets towards pop – up targets of opportunity, as they emerged."[7]

Benjamin goes on to describe a new type of BAS that emerged in Afghanistan. While such BAS had been practiced earlier, it is the scale and regularity with which it was employed, that seems to give it a new hue.

---

[7] Benjamin S. Lambeth, "Air Power Against Terror – America's Conduct of Operation Enduring Freedom". Rand 2006. p. XVI.

Also, as will be seen, such a BAS is easier for air forces, because it obviates the need to identify targets as hostile, since the ground force demanding BAS is already doing so. Operation Enduring Freedom showed that air power can be more effective in many circumstances if it is teamed not only with forward ground spotters but also with friendly ground forces, sufficiently robust to flush out and concentrate enemy forces. What was demonstrated in Afghanistan on repeated occasion, especially early on, was not classic air support or air interdiction, but rather SOF – enabled precision air attacks against enemy ground forces with no friendly ground forces in direct contact.[8]

FAC

The role of FAC has been to guide the strike aircrafts on to the correct target. This is necessitated when own and hostile forces are in close vicinity or engaged in combat and the pilot is unable to distinguish between friend and foe, from air. Guiding the aircrafts, needs crisp and precise language, used with due anticipation, synchronised to strike the aircrafts' speed and manoeuvre. So arises, the need for a fighter pilot to act as an FAC. The target description, and the features leading to the target, needs to be time synchronised with strike aircraft movement. Otherwise the guidance would be gibberish. The FAC also needs to visualise the unfolding panoramic scene as would be seen by the pilot of the fast moving aircraft. Thus, control of strike aircrafts was best done by another strike pilot, sometimes airborne in a slower aircraft or helicopter but mostly situated on the ground, along with army formations. Often, in the absence of a pilot as a FAC, the same control was exercised by an army personnel, trained for the job.

This is how the ground control of a strike aircraft, undertaking BAS, evolved from World War I onwards. But in the last two decades, a lot has changed in the battlefield. Let us briefly review these changes before we consider the control of BAS missions in today's and tomorrow's battlefield.

Today a soldier knows his precise location, thanks to the GPS. The same GPS makes aircraft navigation possible to phenomenally accurate

---

[8] Ibid – Lambeth,p. XXIII

standards, often in singles of metres. The target, marked by ranging devices like the laser is known in precise co-ordinates. The aircraft can be equipped with a GPS guided bombs. The pilot feeds in the GPS coordinates of the target, passed to him, either in voice or data form. And lo and behold, we have the targeting cycle complete, in which the pilot need not see the target, the target spotter need not see and control the strike aircraft. We have very precise BAS capability 24 hours a day, through dark nights or adverse weather, as long as target coordinates can be obtained.

Remove the strike aircraft and put in an armed UAV in its place. Today's UAV – Predator B – can designate the target by its onboard laser and fire the onboard Hellfire missile, to strike the target precisely. If one replaces the Hellfire missile with GPS guided bombs, the same attack cycle can be easily repeated. All this has been happening regularly during Bosnia campaigning in 1995; Kosovo campaign of 1999; and in ongoing operations over Iraq and Afghanistan by NATO forces.

Controlling the aircraft manoeuvre, to make the pilot visually acquire the target is a thing of the past, for a variety of reasons and rightly so. To begin with, it was not that easy to make strike pilots acquire a target, notwithstanding the fact that another pilot in the role of FAC, controlled strike aircrafts. There was no way for FAC to know, when a strike pilot confirmed that he had sighted the target, whether it was the intended target or otherwise – till after the strike had taken place. Next is the aircraft speed. As an aircraft moves, the pilot sees large volumes of airspace go by, in which a small target exists. The pilot gets a fraction of a second to spot the target after perfect guidance from the FAC and exact execution is done by the pilot. Flt Lt Arthur Hughes, when observing IAF air policing operations in NWFP in 1944, observed, "… it is betraying no confidence to say that modern high – speed fighters, like the Hurricane are not ideal for the type of work… Expert opinion up there inclines to the view that what is wanted is something not so fast, very manoeuvrable and with better visibility, an adaptation of the Harvard, perhaps?"[9]

---

[9] Sqn Ldr Rana TS Chinna, " The Eagle Strikes-The Royal Indian Air Force 1932-1950," Ambi Knowledge Resourses Pvt Ltd, New Delhi, 2006. p. 54.

A Harvard files at around 75 – 100 metres/ second. Today, strike aircrafts routinely fly between 250 – 300 metres/ second. A Harvard could turn on the spot, literally. A modern fighter's radius of turn is 4 – 5 kms. So what are the chances of successfully controlling a strike aircraft in order to guide him to spot and attack a tank? And in all probability, the tank would be camouflaged. Will the pilot be able to distinguish between friendly and hostile tanks? It is not that the spirit and the body is not willing. But one cannot overcome the human limitations. An average person can see objects which are within the eye's discernable limits. Ideally, a strike pilot must see the target at least at a distance of 4 km, in order to execute a successful attack. A typical tank measures about 7 metre in length and 3 metres in width. So when seen broadside ON, from a distance of 4 km, its length of 7 metres will subtend an image on the retina, which is less than two milli radians. Whereas, the ability of a six by six human eye, to detect a target is eight milli radians in good light conditions and contrast. Moving tanks give away their positions by dust trails, in the wake. But a stationary tank, that too camouflaged, or buried under sand as in Gulf War – 91 is physically impossible to detect, by the unaided human eye. Magnifying devices cannot be used by a pilot in a single pilot cockpit. Two pilot aircrafts flying at a height may be able to achieve this.[10]

When BAS started initially, the BAS aircraft perforce had to fly low, in order to see the target and to be seen by the FAC. Whereas, BAS which was preplanned, as most of the time by Germans during World War II, the strike aircraft, Stuka would enter a near vertical dive at around 10000' for strike accuracy. To attack in an 85° dive, where gravitational pull accelerates the aircraft, despite idle engine power, and to sight the target, aim correctly to release weapons and also pull out in time, was not easy. So the Stuka had large airbrakes to prevent uncontrolled gravitational acceleration and an automatic recovery system from the dive. Even if the pilot blacked out under high 'G' during pull out, the autopilot would keep them flying safely, till the pilot recovered.

---

[10] A K Tiwary, "Air Power and Counter Insurgency," Lancer Books New Delhi, 2002. p. 127.

All these aircrafts undertaking BAS, fell victim to anti aircraft artillery in large numbers. We saw this typically happen at the Meuse's bridge head to RAF bombers doing BAS. Often this attrition would become unsustainable. To minimise the attrition, allies resorted to SEAD (Suppression of Enemy Air Defence) by launching heavy artillery barrage and integrating the BAS mission with the artillery barrage, hoping that the enemy ack – ack would remain head down. This helped in World War II as it did later in Korea. But this leads to an obvious question – if one has enough organic artillery, then why not use it in the first place, rather than calling for BAS and complicating the situation?[11]

The experience of these wars led to development of a dedicated BAS aircraft by the Americans, the A-10. In Vietnam, between 1965 and 1972, Americans lost 3700 fixed wing combat aircrafts and 4900 helicopters, most of it to ground fire. In addition, Americans had over 15000 helicopters damaged / crashed due ground fire. These were recovered by CH–54 Sky Cranes.[12] Of the above, 66 % of the fixed wing loss and the entire helicopter loss was due to anti aircraft artillery. How did the A-10, the dedicated aircraft for BAS, perform in actual conditions? This test came during Gulf War – 91.

The A-10s were used for FAC role and BAS. The BAS was integrated with SEAD missions. Though MNF had total air superiority, the airspace below 10000' remained highly lethal with Iraqi ack – ack and man portable SAMS. Nearly half the A-10s deployed had serious enough damage requiring major refit. Five were totally lost. After the first 48 hours of the Gulf War 91 experience, US stopped doing BAS from low levels for the rest of the war. Since then, USA has stopped doing BAS from low levels. Now BAS is done from above the lethal envelope of MANPADS and manual ack – ack.

We need to distinguish between reactive BAS to get over a crisis due to enemy offensive and pre-planed BAS to support own offensive. It is

---

11 Lt Col James R Brungees, "Setting the Context –SEAD & Joint War Fighting in Uncertain world ," Air University, Alabama, USA, 1994.

12 A K Tiwary, " Attrition in Air Warfare," Lancer Publishers, New Delhi, 2000, p. 10.

always the latter, which when planned and integrated well, gives results far out of proportion and within controlled attrition, whereas the former is essential to save a fast deteriorating situation. During the 1965 and 1971 Indo-Pak War, Chhamb and Longewala were prime example where adverse and deteriorating situations were restored, by timely BAS. But aircrafts had suffered attrition, which fortunately did not impact them adversely, due to the short duration of the wars.

In the modern battlefield, things are quite different from what it was in the past. As a result, the concept of FAC has also undergone change. In most places, the duties of FAC are undertaken by trained enlisted personnel. The new nomenclature in US forces is listed below:

- USAF – Terminal Attack Controller - Enlisted personnel.

- USMC - Forward Air Controller – Marine soldier.

- SOF - Joint Terminal Attack Controller - SOF personnel.

- USAF / USN/ USMC – Forward Air Controller (air borne)

- FAC (A) - Normally a senior pilot.

We need to review the arrangements for CSFO before examining if maximum benefits of technology have been incorporated into our organisations. Earlier the CSFO organisation that evolved was designed to meet the requirements of a conventional war. The last conventional war we fought was in 1971. Since then, our ground forces have been involved in counter insurgency operations for over two decades in Jammu & Kashmir and at various time in the North East. The Naxal menace, prevalent in over 250 districts, demands much more attention than given so far. The Kargil War of 1999 was fought with many restrictions. Is our existing CSFO organisation up to the mark for current tasks? Do we need any changes in the command and control system to permit greater flexibility to be able to use the same arrangement for most, if not all eventualities? Can we establish pre-decided SOPs to meet different contingencies?

Air Chief Marshal PC Lal, in his memories, described the CAS organisation post World War II as it existed in the IAF. The 65 War brought out the many shortcomings in the same, which were duly attended to, while preparing for the 71 War. Since then not much has changed in the CAS/ CSFO organisation. Of course the increasing complexity of the airspace management has been realised and various joint studies have proposed additions to the earlier organisation. Yet all this has remained only on paper, often even not ratified, for want of additional manpower – which has not been sanctioned. So in situ, what exists today is what existed during the 71 War. It has outlived its equipment and some procedures – as will be evident when we examine experience of nations, actively engaged in recent conflicts. Also we need to notice, how the modern command and control systems have inbuilt flexibility to respond to varying intensities of operations, unlike our system of 71 War vintage. Let us begin with the USA – the leading military power.

USA

The air liaison with the army formations and vice versa exists at multiple levels in the USA, similar to our arrangement – at least theoretically. What has undergone major change in USA is at the functional level, in the field. USAF has JTACs – Joint Tactical Air Controllers, to direct aircraft giving air support. These are enlisted personnel, presently 1200 on active duty as of 2010. Since the demands for them have been continuous due to ongoing wars, USAF plans to double their number in the next four years. These airmen are selected after a pre-screening course. Thereafter, the JTACs undergo training at 'Air Ground Operations School' which is staffed by experienced JTACs. The school is commanded by a Lt Col. The training is 17 weeks long. It is a tough training with a high wash out rate despite the fact that trainees are volunteers who are aware of the glory and the rigour of being a Terminal Attack Controller. These are mostly airmen but also sometimes officer volunteers. The training comprises of rigorous academics in classroom, tough physical training consisting of cross-country runs, up to eight miles ruck marches with up to 45 kgs of load and a rifle. It is followed by training in small unit tactics, combat tactics and five day field training exercises. The studies include security precautions, antenna theory, radio trouble shooting and repair. The TAC duties include establishing and maintaining command and control communication, to control air traffic, naval gunfire, and to provide precision terminal attack guidance to close air support aircraft.[13]

These airmen form a TACP – Tactical Air Control Party, comprising two airmen. TACPs are positioned with the army units as required for operations. The TACP equipment consists of Northrop Gruman MK II Laser Range Finder, having 20 km range. However, the Laser requires many batteries resulting in up to 150 lbs, for all the equipment. Then is the Digital Camera for photographing the target and one can send digital images, using their Radio set. The radio is AN / PRC – 117 F of Harris RF communications. This radio can send digital images by satellite waveform. As we noted earlier, the imagery can be sent to the cockpit directly. If required, the imagery from a cockpit can be sent down to the TACP.

The question arises – does a TACP need 20 km range laser ranger? Lesser the weight – better the mobility. They also have a Raytheon PRC – 113 Have Quick UHF radio. Smoke grenades, Image Intensifiers are additional items with a TACP.

There are a variety of target lasing and designation systems like the CAS Integrated Target System (CITS) by Litton; the Litton Light Weight Laser Designator Range finder; Littons Advanced Laser Targeting System (ALATS). CITS system can pass the target co-ordinates directly to the strike aircraft for a first pass attack. But the target location accuracy being 75 m CEP, at a range of 10 km, raises the question of its usefulness in precision attacks. Will the targets at 10 km range be justifiable for BAS or will BAI be better?

ALATS seems to have been favoured by many customers that include USMC, Norway, Denmark, Israel, Australia, Canada, France, Portugal and Spain, as of 1999.[14] ALATS consists of Ground Laser Target Designator (GLTD), a night sight based on thermal imager or image intensifier and a tripod and tracking mount. The laser has 20 km range. The weight is 5.5kg.

---

[13] http://www2.afsoc.af.mil/news/story.asp?id=12328914 and http://www.airforcetimes. com/news/2010/10/airforce-air-strike-jtac-1008101.

[14] Jane's International Defence Review 9/1999. p. 62.

These are integrated with a suitable modem unit to pass the target info in digital form, to the aircraft.

UK

The TACP concept is quite similar in UK, but there are differences from the US model. UK has a 'Joint FAC Training and Standardisation Unit (JFACTSU). The TACP / FAC in UK is typically composed of an officer, a senior rank and two additional personnel, to act as signaler and driver. Due to shortage of pilots, TACPs are mostly, army or royal marine led.

There are 10 regular primary FAC teams, plus seven reservist primary teams and one standby primary team found from JFACTSU. In each team, there is one primary controller, supported by a secondary controller. In addition, within the army at large, there are more than hundred qualified secondary FACs. Primary controllers are airmen whereas secondary controllers are artillery observers / special forces and army aviation trained for FAC duties.

The normal equipment weight exceeds 45 Kg per person. The communication equipment enables R/T with aircraft; HF Radio for AWACS link; a UHF radio for communication with ground troops; satellite communication with ASOC / CAOC; etc. The diagram below illustrates the communication network.

FAC : Communications

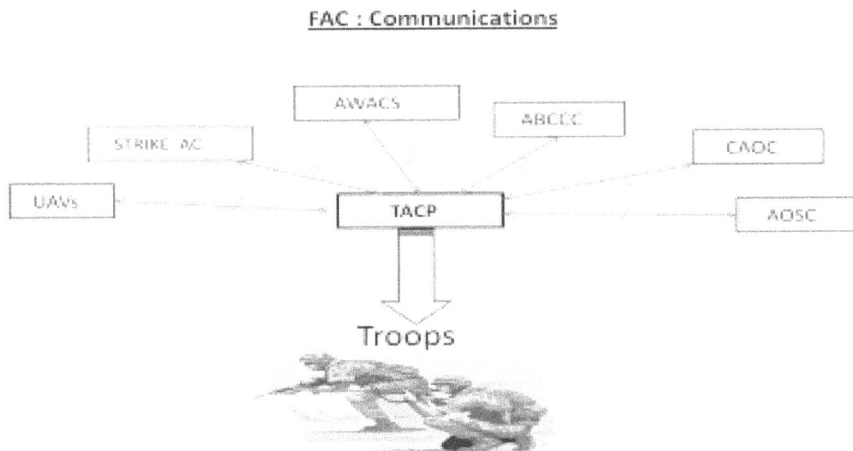

Troops

JFACCTSU consists of seven permanent personnel including the commanding officer, three instructors, two admin corporals and a signal specialist. They run regular courses for FAC training. The course duration is three weeks, followed by practical training. The training includes controlling CAS aircraft, by day and night, both. One analyst indicates need for controlling 36 missions per year, to maintain continuity. Synthetic trainers offer a partial solution. One such is the 'fire support co-ordination and air / ground mission," simulator developed in the Netherlands.[15]

USMC

It is interesting to study USMC organisation for FAC duties, since this is formed by specialised personnel, dedicated for fire control. USMC has a Air Naval Gun Fire Liaison Company. This is a specialist unit of 150 personnel, commanded by a Lt Col. It forms small teams of 4 - 5 men, which are detached to join at Battalion level, to do CAS duties. Air and Naval Gun fire is their only task, during peace and war. This organisation has evolved, based on cumulative experience of pacific theatre Ops during World War II, the wars in Korea, Vietnam, Iraq, Afghanistan etc. The controller is named JTAC – Joint Terminal Attack Controller. A squad has two JTACs for FAC and artillery fire support. One is a Radio operator and the fourth is Squad Automatic Weapon gunner. Their training includes fourteen live missions and three written tests.

This appears to be a good model as it combines professionalism, economy in manpower and centralized overview of personnel. As we will see later, the Indian model is made up of pooled manpower, whose primary bread and butter is far removed from FAC duties, during peacetime. Unless we get war preparation time of six months, as for 71 War, our TACP units will have a difficult time performing even the very basic duties. To be able to exploit the modern technology fully, we need to form dedicated units for the same.

The advances in technology have also addressed the issue of bulky

---

[15] Jane's International Defence Review 9/1999. pp. 55 – 63.

equipment of FAC. Now there is an Advanced Close Air Support System (ACASS) for use. It is a ruggedized hand held computer system, featuring a GPS device, a LASER range finder and a multi – band inter / intra team radio. Area data is provided by fresh imagery from a National Imagery and Mapping Agency Satellite. Data communication is relatively secure because data is transmitted in short bursts. In the aircraft cockpit, aircraft computers automatically process target co-ordinates to weapons and pilots need only to 'Accept / Decline'.[16] Lest one forget, the criteria for BAS controlling was visual observation of target by the FAC. That is why there is a plethora of equipment to observe the target, to be able to direct aircrafts onto it and to avoid fratricide. Earlier this was essential for two reasons – inability to pass the precise location of target and weapon delivery errors. But GPS and precision weapons have brought about revolutionary change. Therefore should not the TACP / FAC also undergo a major change?

When we observe the BAS in recent wars, the following emerges. The old traditional method of a FAC, taking an aircraft flying at low level onto a target is nearly over. Low level has been given up because despite command of air, the inability to suppress proliferating manual ack – ack and MANPADs has made low level, far too lethal. The attrition in such BAS is unsustainable by any air force. Controlling the aircraft to enable the pilot to identify target is not required now, provided accurate target co-ordinates are passed to the pilot / fed into the weapons on UAV. The precise weapons do not err more than 10 -15 metres at worst. And if required, the targets can be indentified from higher levels, using magnifying sensors, on board aircraft. And of course the transparency of the battle field has reduced the uncertainty about targets by an appreciable amount. So the new type of BAS (let us, for the moment call it 'co-ordinates BAS'), has become the norm for modern Air Forces. This BAS is less restrictive and allows pilots enough time to prepare their precise weapons / attack profile, depending upon the weapon. Being outside the envelope of the majority of ack – ack and MANPADS, the pilot is able to concentrate on the job at hand, rather than executing

---

16 Lt Col Stout J. "CAS using Armed UAVs". The Naval Institute's Proceedings, July 2005 at www.military.com/New Content/113190 N1 - 0705 - air – P2,00.htm.

evasive manoeuvres. It is most suitable during night or poor weather/visibility. The FAC need not see the target as long as he can pass accurate target co-ordinates. The target co-ordinates could be observed by FAC himself or obtained by FAC, from sensors of mini tactical UAVs, which are integral to units at the front. The pilot himself need not see the target for GPS guided bombs. The limitations of the human eye no more restrict the successful execution of BAS.

For the same reason, let us review the role of airborne FACs. The airborne FACs came about in World War II itself, to direct the artillery fire. The liaison aircraft of Luftwaffe, operating with the German Army, also fulfilled this role. However, the dedicated airborne FAC, in suitable aircrafts, emerged during the Vietnam War. The tropical country side with dense rain forests and tactics of Vietcong, made it impossible to visually acquire the target by ground based FACs. Hence the airborne FAC in a dedicated FAC aircraft the OV – ID Bronco. This dedicated CAS aircraft was flown by veteran fighter pilots. Many Air Forces happily copied the concept of airborne FAC but being short of aircrafts and funds, used high utility helicopters as the platform. Fortunately for them, they did not have to fight wars – for utility helicopters in modern battlefield will be the first to be shot down. Elevating the FAC was required to see the target hidden to the eyes of a ground based FAC. But the moment this aircraft came into the battle zone, it was subjected to all kinds of fires. Hence the Bronco design will be able to withstand small arms fires.

In today's environment, if UAV can give the target co-ordinates, why should one have airborne FAC? To my mind, days of airborne FAC are over, especially in small aircraft / helicopters. Fast FAC in F-16, during Desert Storm was due to total command of air and preponderance of airpower which is an unusual situation. In our case, the FAC organisation is called Tactical Control Party (TCP). It comprises of a GLO – Ground Liaison Officer and an FAC – typically a fighter pilot. They move around in a jeep/jonga, driven by a dedicated driver, carrying the associated equipment. Normally positioned at Brigade HQ, the team moves to the desired location at expected time of strike. Let us examine each part, if it meets modern day requirement.

The FAC Numbers

Normally each infantry Brigade is supposed to have a FAC. In mountainous areas, due to terrain and lengthy travel time, each Battalion may have a FAC. In armoured formations also, each regiment will require a FAC due to manoeuvre warfare requirements. Indian Army has three Armoured Divisions, four Rapid Divisions, 18 Infantry Divisions, 10 Mechanical Infantry Divisions, 5-7 battalions of Special Forces, and a Para Brigade as fighting formations. These work out to 67 armoured regiments, 30 mechanized battalions, around 319 infantry battalions in 90 brigades, 37 Mountain Infantry Brigades, 1 Para Brigade and 5 – 7 Special Forces battalions. That works out to a total requirement of 230 FACs, that is 230 fighter pilots as FAC, without accounting for sickness, war reserves etc. Whereas in USA TACP is planned at Battalion level and they often support at company level when the need arises. Even in the 1971 war, when we were fortunate to have six months preparation time, IAF had difficulty in mustering so many FACs. Will it be able to do so in future and with little warning? Before we attempt to answer this question let us see the need for fighter pilots as FACs in current times. The best opinions can be gleaned from the war experiences of nations, which are engaged in modern wars.

Benjamin S. Lambeth observed, "the successful insertion of small number of U.S. SOF teams into Afghanistan, after 11 days of bombing, signalled the onset of a new use of air power in joint warfare, in which Air Force terminal attack controllers, working with SOF spotters, positioned forward within line of sight of enemy force concentration directed precision air attacks… These Army SOF troops, with their attached Air Force terminal attack controller, would provide the first eyes on the target, for enabling what eventually became a remarkably successful U.S. exercise in air ground co-operation."[17] Notice there are no fighter pilots as part of TACP. These teams with SOF, often seen during wartime TV coverage, riding the horses in difficult mountainous terrain, while proceeding to their area of operations, underwent proper and thorough joint training before hand. "The combined

---

[17] Benjamin. Ibid. p. XVII

SOF and Air team whose mission was to hunt and kill Scuds in western deserts of Iraq, trained together for six months prior to start of Iraq war 2003. Unprecedented levels of understanding, cooperation and synergy were achieved."[18] Benjamin goes on to state, "perhaps the greatest tactical innovation of the war was highly improvised integration of Air Force terminal attack controllers with Army Special Forces A-Teams and Navy Sea-Air – Land Commando (SEAL) units to produce a SOF–centric application of precision air power against enemy targets...they provided invaluable eyes – on – target identification to U.S. aircrews, for conducting precision air attacks."

As the UAVs' numbers and their employment increases in future, the role and task of FAC will be increasingly taken over by the UAV and its controller, whether we plan it or not. Following incidents from Iraq War 2003, reinforce the above point. "...The potential of UAVs in combat was illustrated by the performance of Britain's relatively unsophisticated Phoenix. On one occasion a sergeant, flying the Phoenix at its maximum range of 60 km, spotted a concentration of Iraqi soldiers and vehicles. On his own initiative, even though he had no experience as a forward air controller, he called in an F-18 aircraft to strike the Iraqis. Other Phoenix operators called down mortar and artillery fire on concentrations of enemy troops. In one case they used the Phoenix and artillery fire to destroy Iraqi naval craft, operating in the Shatt al Arab water way.[19] When we say today's battlefield is more transparent, it means that location and number of enemy troops deployed is more visible – and the precise location of visible forces is available, thanks to the GPS technology, combined with laser making/ designation. Towards this, the UAVs accounted for much of the improved sensor capabilities. But the war also suggested that the full potential of UAVs has not been reached.[20] Yet another incident reinforces the above argument. "On the evening of April 04, a marine Hunter UAV picked up the

---

[18] Gp Capt RM Poole, Ibid. p. 11.

[19] William Murray & Maj Gen Robert H. Scales, Jr, "The Iraq War – A Military History" Natraj Publishers, Dehradun 2006. p. 16.

[20] Ibid. p. 163.

movement of a substantial number of Iraqi tanks and artillery pieces, as they attempted to deploy out of the capital, under the cover of darkness. The senior watch officer in 3rd Marine Aircraft Wings combat operation centre, forwarded the coordinates to Harriers and F/A – 18 Hornets overhead. The resulting attack destroyed approximately eighty vehicles and killed a number of Iraqis."[21] If the above build up had not been detected in time by UAV, it would have resulted in crisis in immediate air support. Secondly, because the enemy forces were detected well away from own FLOT, it was easy to decide, to engage the enemy, for the duty officer because there was no need for detailed coordination with his own troop's movement and fire. It would not be out of place to remember that in the Battle of Al Khafji during Gulf War – 91, once again the Iraqi armour was spotted by JSTARS, well before it came in contact with MNF troops. At it's depth location itself, the Iraqi armour was destroyed in BAI missions.

This brings us to another important point, regarding delegation and decentralized decision making. Put in another way, it is the need for good situational awareness at all levels and ability and confidence to make decisions against emerging targets. Murray observers, "what was particularly impressive about air power in the Iraq war was the ability of the command and control system, to retarget aircrafts in the air and assign them new targets, that had only recently popped up from UAV or other sensors. That capability approached real – time targeting and allowed the coalition to attack the enemy, as he began to move. Yet, the very communication capabilities that enabled such flexibility can be used for top-down control rather than true, real-time execution. Dangerous tendencies in this direction remain alive and well in the American military…"[22]

In our command and control review, we need to address this issue, if we are to capitalize on modern air power for real time targeting. The SOPs have to be arrived at, in peace time or else we will not be utilising the full potential of modern Air power.

---

[21] Ibid. pp. 173 – 174.

[22] Ibid Murray, pp. 182 – 183.

Future Air to Ground Weapons and BAS

We noted that earlier the strike aircrafts needed to come low and attack in order to improve weapon accuracy. Now the precision weapons obviate the need to fly low. Also the aircraft controlling is reduced to passing correct target co-ordinates. Let us briefly see some of the latest air to ground precision weapons and the likely weapons in future, to relate it with the need and amount of FAC controlling.

Co-ordinate Guided Weapons

The USAF defines precision weapons as those that achieve a CEP of 3 metres or less.[23] Near precision weapons are those that achieve a CEP of 13 metres or less. Weapons which navigate to target coordinates, using INS are called co-ordinates guided weapons. INS – only guidance, either by design or degradation, is built to achieve a CEP of 30 metres or less. By providing nearly the same accuracy as current precision munitions, but in all weather conditions, co-ordinate guided weapons make high levels of accuracy continuously available to the commanders. The relatively low cost of near precision, and its navigational process, make it possible to employ large numbers.[24] A coordinate guided weapon has an INS system in the tail kit. The pilot feeds in the target coordinates in three dimension. The aircraft navigation system as well as the GPS receiver provides its current position. The tail assembly steers the weapon towards the target. The weapon range depends upon aircraft altitude. Higher the altitude, greater is the range. This range can be further increased by attaching mini wings to the weapon, which improves its glide ratio.

The Joint Direct Attack Munitions (JDAM), the Wind Corrected Munitions Dispensers (WCMD) and the Joint Standoff Weapon (JSOW) are co-ordinate guided weapons in use with USAF and some more Air

---

[23] US Air Force Weapons School, "SSS 600 A : Introduction to Precision Guided Munitions,". Nellis AFB, Nevada, Mar 2003

[24] Maj Jeffrey B. Taliaferro, "Coordinate – Guided Weapons in Close Air Support : An Evaluation of Risk," Air University, Alabama. 2003. p. 4.

Forces. WCMD has a CEP of 30 metres or less and is only an INS guided weapon. With mid course GPS update, this CEP is improved to 13 metres or less. JSOW also has a CEP of 13 metres or less.

Earlier, Laser bombs also had an accuracy of around 13m CEP. Coordinate-guided bombs are similar in cost as earlier laser bombs or cheaper ones, each bomb being around $200,000 in 2003 US dollars. The accuracy of coordinate – guided weapons can be increased by fitting Imaging Infra Red seekers in the nose, for final guidance, reducing errors to 3m CEP and less. Examples of such weapons were LOCAAS – Low Cost Autonomous Attack System, BAT – Brilliant Anti Tank Sub munitions, being developed to counter Soviet armoured formations during Cold – War era. However, these have been put on hold after considerable research, since presently no such threat is forecast. But the technology is available and could be weaponised, whenever the need arises. The following are the operational precision weapons in use.

Small Diametre Bomb (SDB). It is a small diametre bomb weighing 285 lbs but packs the explosive power of a 2000 lb due advanced explosive. It has a warhead of a 50 lb high explosive which can penetrate 1.8 metres of reinforced concrete. Fitted with JDAM kit i.e., steerable tail unit, it has a CEP of 10 m, using GPS signals for position updates and INS, navigating the bomb to the specified target co-ordinates. It has a range of 72 -108 km. Each bomb rack can carry four SDBs and especially built racks can carry 12 SDBs. It was introduced into USAF in Jan 2006.

There is an enhanced version, SDB II (Spiral 2) also planned to be used against both static and mobile targets. It's planned CEP is 3 m. This enhancement in CEP will be achieved by fitting a low cost terminal seeker to the SDB. A B2 Bomber successfully released 80 JDAMs against 80 separate targets on a single pass on 10 Sep 03. This number was planned to be increased to 200 bombs!

SDB MK III is planned as a WASAMM – Wide Area Search Autonomous Attack Miniature Munitions. The development is going on.

WCMD – Wind Corrected Munitions Dispenser. There were a variety of cluster bombs in USAF, like the CBU 87, CBU 97 etc. These numbered around 40000. However during Gulf War – 91, after the first 24 hours, USAF took a conscious decision to stop low level attacks, due to unsustainable attrition rate to Iraqi manual ack – ack and MANPADS. But the cluster bombs had been designed to be released only at low level to utilise their shot gun effect of area coverage.[25] To be able to release them from attitudes, USA developed WCMD. The WCMD would allow release at high altitudes; correct the Bomb for wind drift and then allow it to function at low level, as planned earlier. So the cluster bomb with WCMD is a weapon presently in use as well for future battle field. It has INS and GPS for navigation. It carries 10 BLU – 108 sub munitions, each sub munition having four bomblets.

Sensor Fused Weapons (SFW). It is a weapon with 40 smart sub munitions. As it descends, it corrects for winds with a tail kit, fitted for this purpose. A laser range finder enables it to compute the correct range. Each sub-munition has an IR Sensor, that can distinguish and home on to an armoured vehicle. To be able to do this slowly, the sub munition spirals down on a parachute. Once it locates the target, then it discards the parachute and attacks the tank. The above weapons are deadly for a static target. These weapons as well as other such weapons are being developed further, against mobile targets. LOCAAS was one such example.

Field Artillery – Present & Future

In order to comprehend fire integration on the battlefield, it is necessary to see what all organic fire power is available with Armies. When CAS initially started during World War I, apart from the fire from the Infantry weapons, the artillery provided long range fire power. Its effective range was around 5 km. So CAS integration with 5 km range artillery was relatively a simple thing. In comparison, today's battlefield has far more organic weapons.

Typically, modern Armies have mortars, howitzers, artillery – towed or mobile, Multiple Rocket Launchers (MLRs), and the tactical missiles. These weapons have different ranges, extending as much as 300 km in case of

---

[25] Fuse Considerations. The fuse was only for low levels.

Prithvi II and Brahmos Cruise Missiles. All these weapons are meant to provide necessary fire support. The US Army provides a definition of fire support, that specifically links aircraft and artillery. It defines fire support as:

"Fire support is the collective and coordinated use of lethal and non – lethal fires, in a responsive, integrated, and synchronised manner, to achieve the maximum desirable effects against ground targets, in support of operational and tactical combat operations, and to prevent or minimise fratricide and undesirable collateral damage. Lethal fires include armed aircraft and land-based and sea-based indirect fire systems (Such as field artillery, mortars and naval surfaces fires). Non – lethal fires include electronic warfare capabilities, psychological operations, the use of munitions such as illumination and smoke, and non – lethal, area-type delivery systems that employ water, sticky / slickly agents, and similar materials. Desirable effects are those that directly support the commander's objectives and operational schemes, and that comply with his guidance and intent for fire. They achieve a specified purpose in time and space.[26]

Now we can also add to the above list the unmanned armed aerial system like Predator B, which seem to be doing maximum fire support in Afghanistan. The typical range of these weapons is shown below diagrammatically. Its relevance will be appreciated when we talk of FLOT, FEBA, FSCL, Bomb line etc.

---

[26] U.S Army Field Manual 3 – 9, Doctrine for Fire Support Final Draft (Washington : US Government Printing Office, 2002. p. 1-2)

Artillery:Modern Battle Field

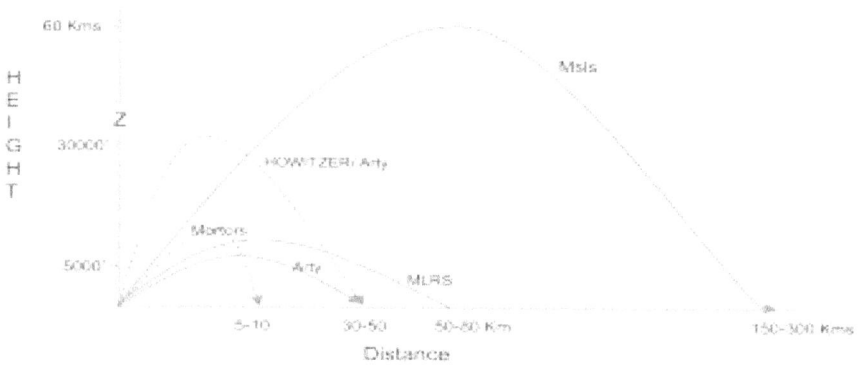

The ranges and altitudes are general and simplistic for ease of understanding. The actual figures would represent a far more complex battle space. Now imagine integration in real time, of all these fires with UAVs, and other air space users, transiting the battle space? To add to all this, the CAS and BAI aircraft giving fire support in the battlefield..

So what is the type and quality of fire power available to an army commander placed directly under command? Is it potent enough to make requirements of CAS redundant? How much organic fire power must be put on "Hold Fire" to permit a CAS aircraft / UAV to provide needed fire support? Is it worth the penalty of silencing organic fire power? While exact answers would emerge by making a matrix of exact ranges, terminal accuracies and maximum altitude reached by the projectiles for various weapon system, for our study, we shall assume general average figures, not too far removed from reality.

By and large, field artillery remains an area restricted weapon when compared to modern precision guided munitions. Its accuracy is improved, over time, by a system of fire, observe, correct and re-fire, against static targets. There are some precision munitions like the 'Copper head' in USA and 'Krasponal' in Russia. The projectiles from these systems, require laser illumination of the target to home on to it. Which means that at the end of the projectiles' flight path there must be someone to illuminate the target. Detailed coordination is required between firing unit and the illuminator – a rarity in an intense battle field. Another one, the M 898 Sense and Destroy Armor Munitions (SADRAM) provides a capability for precision engagement of lightly armoured vehicles. In addition, Excalibur (XM 892) is a 155 mm precision guided artillery round, using GPS. Its range is 50 km with a CEP of 10 m.

Among the MLRS, M 270 AI of USA can fire twelve rockets at twelve separate aim points or two missiles at two aim points in less than two minutes. These are GPS guided. The ATACMS (Advanced tactical missile) Block I has a range of 165 km, while the GPS- guided Block 1A has a range greater than 300 kms. The Block II carries 13 Brilliant Anti Tank (BAT) rounds, that reach a range of 140 kms. BAT sub – munitions is an aerodynamically stable "glider" that employs passive acoustic and infrared sensors to find, attack and destroy tanks.[27]

Now let us peep into the future – say another 10 yrs, because from request for proposal to operational induction, the process often takes 10 yrs or more, on an average. Suppose the Corp Commander in 2020 has under command, an Armed UAV Squadron, allotted from Command HQ / Army HQ. In 2020, a UAV is likely to have operational persistence of 48 hrs, is likely to have 8–10 Small Diametre Bombs / air to ground Hell fire missiles, etc. Along with the organic fire power, most of it, GPS guided and precise, this armed UAV would be on call 24 hrs, fulfilling the role of CAS UAV. A squadron of UAV would permit constant UAV cover. It will be highly affordable, compared to say, the cost of CAS by modern combat aircraft, 24 hrs a day, for many days. Being unmanned, integration of UAV will pose far lesser problems of fire integration and air space usage. I am not against CAS by manned aircraft. But the trend is already moving towards this unmanned CAS. If the battlefield of the future is anything like this, then we seriously need to review our CSFO procedures.

So let us peep into the future of CSFO in our scenario. Our borders in

---

[27] David A. Lee, pp. 70 -75.

the west and north will remain contentious. They involve an extremely long distance of about 6000 km. CSFO could be required in the deserts, in the plains of Punjab as well as in the hills and mountains. The Himalayan heights, exceeding 20000 feet at some of the places, will adversely affect the trajectories of conventional weapons. The aerodynamic instability, a result of weapons like guns and rockets, would adversely affect the fighter's engine as happened during the Kargil War. The CSFO requirement could be simultaneous, at many places far apart, especially in a two front war. Over and above this, the war on terror would require sporadic CSFO strikes along with near continuous ISR, always and all the year round. This would be by day and night. Precision weapons would be needed to minimise collateral damage; to overcome errors due to thin atmosphere at the Himalayan heights; to reduce the numbers of sorties, thereby aircrafts having to meet vast demands at places far apart, near simultaneously. Lesser sorties for the same task means lesser attrition. That is, precise weapons will be far more economical than what their procurement cost might suggest at first glance. The lion's share of the task would be by UCAVs. Therefore, we need to refine our doctrines, operational directives and SOPs. We need to update our equipment and training.

7

CYBER WARFARE

Some contemporary thinkers have equated Cyber-Warfare as another new form of warfare, which is at par with Land, Naval and Air Warfare. This is partly reflected in USA, creating a new Cyber Command to be headed by a General, who will also be the boss of Central Security Services and Director of National Security Agency. In the 2010 strategic review of security and defence in UK, while many major defence programmes have been cut and overall defence budget is reduced by 8 percent, the cyber war has been allotted £ 650 m for the period 2010–14. A significant increase indeed.

While cyber war seems a very familiar term to everyone, it will be useful to revisit its characteristics, which make it so important and so different from other forms of warfare. It is distinctly different from the traditional warfare wherein Armies, Navies and Air Forces are massed against each other, to fight one another.

Cyber war can be fought by any one; even an individual using his hacking skills against huge corporations, nations or even different civilizations. One single person's malicious software can wreck havoc on computers' networks and programmes, spread across nations and continents. The modern world's industry, economy, institutions and every other facet of life is supported by computers and associated software. So all these facets of life can be disrupted and often for prolonged periods, by cyber attacks. The individual could be acting alone; he could be part of a group, pursuing its inimical agenda or could be state supported, working to further the plans of the state. The defender cannot distinguish between them or pinpoint the full identity of the attacker or the actual source of attack. So while the cyber enemy may be guessed, definite pinpointing is nearly impossible.

Amongst various types of warfare, cyber war is the cheapest option. At its simplest, all it requires is one individual on one computer to originate cyber attacks. There is no need for regular massive cyber armies, equipped with all the paraphernalia of a conventional war, being trained, sustained and replenished regularly. Unlike the conventional war, where the attacker generally suffers heavy casualties, in cyber war, there is no casualty to the attacker. Here it is not the physical might of a soldier, the quality and quantity of equipment, the integration and orchestration of system of systems, or the strategic genius of a General which is tested. But it is only the computer genius and skills – and these too come as easily to gifted teens as to the experts after years of serious study and perseverance. Therefore, each and everyone cannot be a cyber warrior. Conscription would not do to create a cyber army. It is created by recruiting suitable people with aptitude for such work. In cyber force, there is not much place for the officer – soldier hierarchy. Rather it is more akin to the team of the like minded.

When one's computer system does not work, it is not easy to distinguish whether the failure is a genuine malfunction or a result of malicious attack. More often then not one tends to believe that his computer system itself is malfunctioning. So it is difficult to determine if one is under cyber attack. The nature of attacks are such, for example hidden Trojans activated on command or at some pre-determined time, so that one does not know when the actual attack was launched.

The origins of attack also remain uncertain. The attacking nation or non-state actor can route his attack via computers, located in a third country or even through benign computers, based in the country being attacked. These could be the personal computers of citizens of the country under attack. Such an approach poses major dilemma for the defender and for the right to computer privacy in democratic societies.

The malware can be inbuilt in to the computer system at the manufacturing stage itself. It can be pre designed in micro chips for various items like sensors, routers, switches etc. It can be injected later on into the system as a sleeper cell. It's algorithm can be programmed in a variety of ways, to defeat most defences.

The defender in cyber world has to cope with many problems. The existing defences are against only known viruses / worms. Defence network, therefore, requires constant upgradation. Even secure nets can be injected with virus even though the attacker is not physically connected to the net. One can provide many layers of security but excessive security on the net decreases the system's speed. Information on cyber war is difficult to find. However, certain amount of information is available about cyber war in USA, in the open literature. Hence it is proposed to study the evolution of cyber war in USA.

USA

Electronic Warfare(EW) started during World War II. The EW matured as the radars and radar guided SAMs and anti-aircraft artillery evolved through the Vietnam war, the wars in the Middle East etc. Till recently, EW meant brute jamming of signals or breaking the electronic lock on an aircraft, by moving the lock away spatially. In the Op Desert Storm of Gulf War 91, false target information was injected into Iraqi Integrated Air Defence System, thereby misleading its computers. This can be considered the start of cyber war in the military domain. The cyber war in the civil domain, by way of unethical hacking into banking networks, started around the same time or a little earlier.

So now there are three terms: EW, Cyber War and Information War often loosely used to convey the same thing. Electronic war is said to take place when electrons in a system are disturbed. Cyber space is also the space where electrons flow, conveying information. But cyber space is normally referred to space in which computer electrons move around – either within the computer itself or between many computers connected in a network. The network itself could be a cable or fibre optic network or a wireless net in which electronic signals move between a transmitter and a receiver. The most apt example would be a satellite and its terminals. Thus, in the militaries too, initially terms like EW, IW and Cyber war were used loosely and interchangeably.

Cyber war has become a major subset of warfare now, because the militaries and their equipments rely on many systems, each of which has computers, often many computers in each system. At the same time, all facets of civil life, industry, banking and financial services, power generation etc. have also been based on extensive computer networks and infinite number of software lines. In such a huge complex of electrons, EW as practiced till 1980s, forms a small subset. Altering cyber electrons, means altering information–hence the term IW. However, in current US terminologies, IW means irregular warfare. Cyber war includes the earlier EW and IW.

Evolution of Cyber War

USAF set up IW squadrons in 1980s. The banking institutions and major industries, especially the Aero Space industries also started building in cyber security in their networks. The financial institutions were at the forefront of cyber attacks, wherein hackers tried to steal / siphon away money. This threat to banks and the security precautions could not be made public, in order to retain the investor confidence.

As a result of success of IW in the Gulf War - 91, USAF decided on IW across full spectrum of command and control. So the 688th Information Operations Wing was set up. The Wing has technical skill sets of AF Electronic Warfare centre; AF Cryptographic support centre's Securities directorate and Intelligence capabilities from former AF Intelligence Command. As in 2010, it has a staff of 1000, which includes military and civil staff.

In 1993, USAF established an IW Cell at Kelly Air Force Base Texas. By mid 90s, the IW flight, consisting of 25 personnel, would work alongside CAOC, whenever operations were going on. IW operations were undertaken during Bosnia Operation in 1995 and against Serbia in 1999. The comprehensive operations included EW against Radars and SAMs, cyber attacks against IADS, operations against Television, Radio as well as cyber attacks against computer based systems like power generation, Oil refining systems etc.

In the past, USA has caused a massive explosion in a new trans-

Siberian oil pipeline, running from the Urengoi gas fields in Siberia across Kazakhstan, Russia and Eastern Europe. The pipeline software that was to run the pumps, turbines, and valves was programmed to go haywire, after a decent interval, to reset pump speeds and valve settings to produce pressures far beyond those acceptable to the pipeline joints and welds.[1] USN established its cyber cell in 1999 and mandated the unit to become like the 'Top Gun' amongst fliers.

In Dec 1998, DoD / USAF established Joint Task Force on Computer Network Defence JTF – CND. It was headed by a Maj Gen and was to work with Army, Navy and Marine Corps. This was an immediate result of a massive malware attack on US military nets. It took the US, 14 months to clean up this virus, termed Solar Sunrise from its systems, numbering more than 500. It also revealed the enormity of the possible damage that can be caused to improperly secure networks.

Cyber War exercises named "Eligible Receiver' and "Solar Sunrise' were conducted in which Federal Agencies/Services, Israeli analysts and Californian teens attacked Defence networks. Weaknesses and vulnerabilities were identified and preventive steps initiated. In Sep 2001, Pentagon created Joint Task Force - Computer Network Operations - JTF-CNO. Computer Network Operations(CNO) replacing CND implied need to attack, in order to defend proactively.

In 2008, DoD defined cyber space as, "a global domain within the information environment consisting of interdependent network of information technology infra structures, including the Internet, telecommunication network, computer systems, and embedded processor and controllers." It illustrated that cyber space has data, networks and electronic devices. Good cyber defence implies protecting all three components and not merely data. Earlier it was believed that encrypting data was enough for cyber security. Cyber Defence now meant the following:

1. Secure all exclusive networks in which individuals cannot plug in Pen

---

[1] Thomas C. Reed, " At the Abyss - An Insider's History of the Cold War," Ballantine Books, New York, 2004. p. 268

Drives, CDs and external devices.

2. Defence in depth by fire walls, so that when under a cyber attack the system degrades gradually rather than a catastrophic collapse and after the attack is over, the system recovers.

3. The system should be Self Diagnosing and have built in healing capability.

4. Databases must employ stealth methodologies where for example, modulating chip technology enables then to hide, morph and masquerade, as effectively as any attacking agent.[2]

Cyber security is akin to Air Superiority. One has to fight to attain it and thereafter sustain it with constant effort. Also Cyber security relates to place and time. Unlike Air war in which offense is the best defence, in Cyber War, defence becomes primary because of the nature of the attacker. There are no hostile cyber bases, which preemptive bombing can destroy.

In 2001, USAF placed the Cyber Wing under Space Command. By May 2002, it had a manning of 340 personnel. Later, Cyber Command was made a sub unit of US Strategic command. It achieved full operational capability on 31 Oct, 2010. The Cyber Command is headed by a General, who also is the Director of National Security Agency (NSA) and Chief of Central Security Services. This arrangement in one stroke has made cyber structure more horizontal and integrated. Cyber command looks after all military networks, numbering 15000 in all the Services. It has replaced the earlier Joint Task Force – Computer Network Operating and the Joint Functional Component Command for Network Warfare JFCC – NW. It has under it, the Cyber Commands of the US Army, Navy, Marine Corps and Air Force. It is responsible for both defence and offense, in Cyber War. In addition, it provides technical and electronic warfare support, to Department of Homeland Security (DHS). If and when asked by DHS, it will provide additional assistance. DHS looks after civil and private networks.

---

[2] "USAF Strategy – Past, Present & Future 2018 – 2023" AF Research Institute, 2008. Gen John A. Shaud Ph.D Air University, Jan 2009. pp. 45 – 50.

NSA looks after all the government networks apart from the ones in military domain. US CYBERCOM has been tasked to develop:

1. Methods to assess operational impact of intrusions.

2. Identify proper response.

3. Co-ordinate action with appropriate organisations.

4. Prepare Response Plans.

5. Execute plans through Service components.

US CYBERCOM will also issue Operational Alert conditions, depending upon detected threats. The conditions are normal, A, B, C & D. Over and above these arrangements, the Cyber organisations seek support and rely on private security specialist companies, to deal with cyber threat.

The earlier concept of cyber security was purely defensive. However, as the cyber process and attacks kept increasing, especially post 09/11 and after the incident of US spy plane, P3C Orion's collision with a Chinese interceptor, in which the Chinese pilot died, USA selected a new strategy for cyber security. Now it was felt that purely defensive strategy was reactive and insufficient to ward off cyber threat. For proper cyber security, there is a need to actively patrol the cyber network, for detecting potential trouble. So the new strategy of cyber attack comprises of the following:

(a) Denial of Service

(b) To patrol the Internet to pinpoint attackers.

(c) To create Logic bombs, worms, Trojans & Malware for use as and when needed.

The following diagram illustrates the working of a computer network attack (CNA).[3]

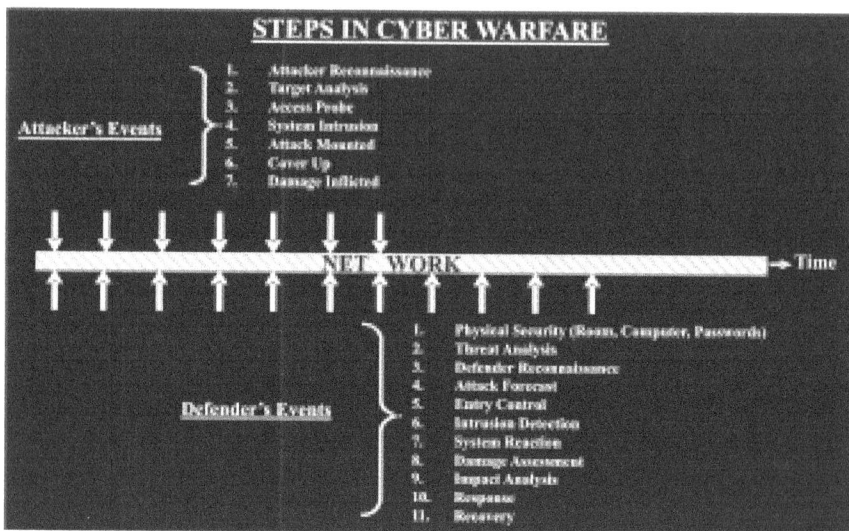

STEPS IN CYBER WARFARE

Attacker's Events
1. Attacker Reconnaissance
2. Target Analysis
3. Access Probe
4. System Intrusion
5. Attack Mounted
6. Cover Up
7. Damage Inflicted

NET WORK → Time

Defender's Events
1. Physical Security (Room, Computer, Passwords)
2. Threat Analysis
3. Defender Reconnaissance
4. Attack Forecast
5. Entry Control
6. Intrusion Detection
7. System Reaction
8. Damage Assessment
9. Impact Analysis
10. Response
11. Recovery

Rivet Joint is an specialist transport aircraft (KC-135) which is used for CNA. It is in contact with agencies like NSA, JTF – CNA, and IW – EW centres, via satellite links to receive and send back latest information for CNA planning. It injects cyber weapons as appropriate into hostile IADS networks, Scud type missiles command and control centres and the communication networks. Another special aircraft called Compass Call (C-130 modified) monitors the effectiveness of communication network attacks.

---

[3] AWST 04 Nov 2002. p. 32.

CYBER ATTACKS

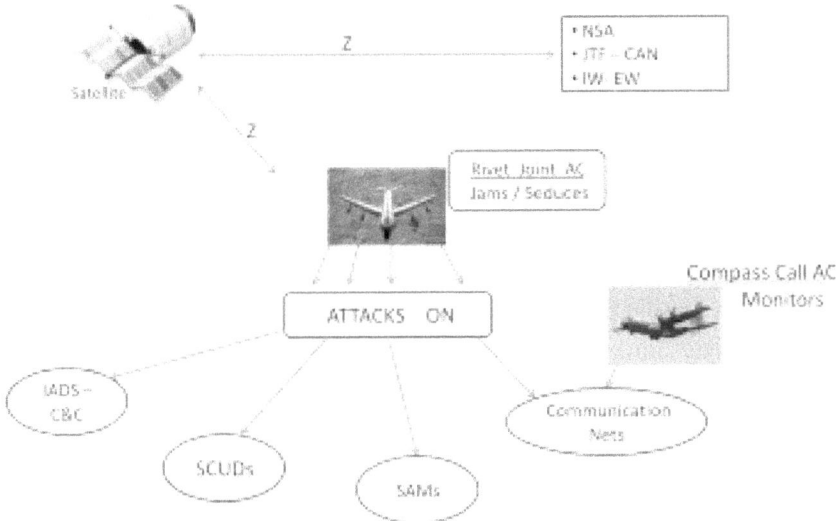

In USA, the 24th AF looks after cyber operations, manned by 14000 airmen, the 24th AF has three major wings and an operations centre under it. These are:

(a) **67th Network Warfare Wing**: It looks after information operations. It's 8000 strong manpower is located at some 100 locations, world wide. There are 35 squadrons and these deal in operations of Television, Radio, Telephone exchange and networks, including mobile phones and networks.

(b) **688th Information Operation Wing**: Deals in cyber space R&D and is manned by about 1000 members of staff, which is a mix of the military and civil.

(c) **689th Combat Communication Wing**: It's mission is to train, deploy and deliver expeditionary and specialised communication; air traffic and landing systems for relief and combat operations.

In 2010, USAF undertook some important steps with regard to the cyber branch. It established a new cadre for cyber war, with 1000 cyber warriors. These personnel were selected after a strict screening process, which also judged their aptitude for cyber work. Their performance in online games was also a major criteria. This cadre is to be expanded to 6000. The cadre will comprise of military, government employees, contractors and willing patriotic youths. Specialist cyber strike units will be created from these personnel. The training will include undergraduate cyber training and Initial qualification training. The standards of evaluation and examinations will follow similar pattern as for flying training. The cyber warriors will get incentive pay similar to flying pay. Their main communication devices will be Droids and I Phones, connected on secure and non-secure networks.

The cyber warriors will identify own networks' weaknesses, which will be followed up by regular patch up of vulnerabilities. In addition, their actual target could include blowing up electric generators/motors; use of high power microwave, to upset fly by control of combat aircraft and more.[4]

The NSA and JFCC – NW have worked together since 2005. The NSA has 700 personnel with Ph.Ds. This vast experience is shared by the other cyber warriors, who have benefited immensely. The CYBERCOM has partnerships with 100 universities, to train students on net security. Many of these students, thereafter, join NSA or civil cyber agencies. Now using the computer net attack, US forces can penetrate hostile computers' systems and either mine it for data or damage it with crippling algorithms or even spoof it with false information. Some of the CNA tricks include ringing hostile phones every 30 seconds; sending a fabricated Fax directly to the enemy operator to do things that would lead to trouble; sending accusatory e-mails etc. The idea is to make the enemy distrust his own communication system or to shut down all communications.[5]

The Israelis established an Umbrella C4 I in Mar 2003. By 2007, all intelligence networks were connected, sharing all sensor information. The

---

[4] AWST 05 Apr 2010. pp. 48 – 51.
[5] AWST 05 Apr 2004. p. 48.

network includes fixed sites as well as mobile sites. During the 2009 Gaza conflict, the Israeli Air Force downloaded sensor imagery on Youtube; its tweets warned of rocket attacks and it used 'help-us-win.com' blog to mobilise public support[6].

Placed at *Appendix* are the recommendations with respect to cyber war, by a USAF study in 2008. The study was undertaken to suggest needed reorganisation within the USAF for the 2018 – 2023 time frame. Cyber war is a new domain for all the countries. It appears that USA and China have a lead of about ten years, over India, in the cyber war domain. The emphasis placed by them on cyber war, is instructive for us to take note of.[7]

Little is revealed about cyber defences in most countries. India is no exception. The press reports of the past however, suggest that the cyber domain and its security has got the government's attention, at the highest level. Sufficient attention has been devoted towards this aspect. Still it would be worthwhile to re-examine some of the issues listed below in contemporary context.

We should hasten towards automation and digitisation slowly. Rather than digitising each and everything we should proceed only on a need basis. This would minimise unnecessary exposure in the cyber world. We should have intra-nets within organisations. Whether all the nets should be connected is a moot point. Interconnecting should be strictly on need basis. It should not be a blind policy to connect all nets, irrespective of the need.

Doctrinally, there is no reason as to not proceed, following the US model. Defence alone is incapable of providing sufficient cyber security. Multiple options are required depending upon the security classification of the net. Therefore, advantages of the offensive cyber policies must be explored and integrated, as needed.

---

[6] In a Speech by Chief of RAF, at Information Superiority Conference, 2010.

[7] John A. Shaud Ph.D, General, USAF, Retired "In Service to the Nation – Air Force Research Institute Strate gic Concept for 2018 – 2023." Air Univercity Press, Maxwell Air Force Base Alabama, Jan 2009.

Cyber manning requires a new approach, quite different from the prevailing one so far. It needs a balanced mix of gifted youngsters and highly qualified cyber experts. They need to work in flexible ways, different from conventional organisations. Hesitation and conservatism will retard progress in the cyber field.

Appendix
(Refers page 109)

Cyberspace: Boundless Opportunity and Significant Vulnerabilities

(a) USAF must not focus solely on protecting its databases, but rather it must also protect its networks and the functioning of electronic devices to enable cyberspace control.

(b) USAF must be prepared to conduct warfare in cyberspace to secure the domain at the time and place of its choosing.

(c) Call for an interagency commission to resolve the issues of jurisdictional authority and, if needed, author legislation for title 10 revision.

(d) While offense offers a distinct advantage for airpower, deterrence and defence must become co-equal propositions in cyberspace.

(e) Reclaim the internet, moving to a closed network, one that does not allow interaction with its civilian counterpart in any capacity or other open systems, across the DOD.

(f) View cyberspace holistically, developing organisations and tactics to defend them, regardless of location, while retaining freedom of action for our forces.

(g) Develop system resiliency, with a layered defence in depth, that reacts to threats and sets in motion procedures for post – attack recovery.

(h) Develop and field self – diagnosing and self – healing systems with adequate redundant capacity for survivability.

(i) Develop systems to support real – time Cyberspace Situational Awareness (CSA)

(j) Develop a new corps of professionals, capable of waging cyber warfare.

(k) Develop a structured professional development curriculum with a UCT school that provides the needed military education, required for newly minted second lieutenants.

(l) Create a National Cyberspace Studies Institute (NCSI) that provides an increased understanding of cyber operations, appropriate for success at the advanced ranks.

(m) Ensure adequate pay, attendance at the right schools – PME and weapons school – and promotion.

(n) Find a home / advocate for future cyber – warriors, one equal to that of air / space.

(o) Identify Guard and Reserve billets for cyber – professionals who are separate from active duty.

(p) Develop a construct to incorporate Guard and Reserve into the "fight", either through stand – alone units or as a part of active duty units.

(q) Develop a Cyberspace Red Team to probe DOD networks and provide input for offensive, defensive, and counter offensive strategies.

(r) Develop an industry council, where senior military and industry representatives convene to establish requirements and propose technological solutions.

(s) Partner with the private sector – universities and commercial industries, to properly leverage American expertise.

8

UAV OPERATIONS

IAF started the UAV path fairly early in comparison to other important elements, necessary for a modern Air Force. For example, nearly 15 Air Forces had been operating AWACS/AEW&C for years, before IAF contemplated its procurement. Same was the case with air refuellers. In fact, Jaguars inducted in 1979 as deep penetration strike aircraft had their air to air refuelling capability removed to fulfil the Indian requirement! In the case of UAVs, fortunately this undue delay did not occur. So now, IAF has nearly 14 years of experience in UAV operations.

A study of UAV operations in other Air Forces reveals following points which could merit attention in our review of UAV operations and its integration in overall operations – singly, jointly and within civil airspace for air space management.

The first major point is the selection and training of UAV operators. Basically medium and large endurance UAVs have an External Pilot (EP) who launches / conducts the take off and does the recovery and landing of the UAV. An Internal Pilot (IP), thereafter flies/ operates the UAV itself. It could be local operations or operations half way around the world; example being USAF UAVs in Afghanistan and Iraq, being operated from CONUS. Then there are payload operators who operate the various pay loads dealing with imagery, signals, EW etc.

Nearly all Air Forces started using aircraft and helicopter pilots as EP and IP. IP also often acted as the overall Mission Commander. As numbers of UAVs increased, the Air Forces faced the problem of shortage of pilots. USAF experienced similar problems as they developed space operations. Initially only engineering qualified officers operated satellites. Later they were successfully able to induct non - science background officers for space operations as well as enlisted personnel for routine space functions. Now similar models are being looked into for UAV operations. Today the USAF is training more number of UAV pilots than normal pilots.

There is no doubt that UAVs will continue to form increasingly larger proportion of Air Forces in the future. Therefore, it is necessary to develop a separate operational career field for the UAV operators. There is need to select UAV pilots, based on what is needed for UAV operations. While this will be similar to requirements as for pilot selection, there will be additional criteria for UAV pilots. The RAF and the USAF, since 2009 are experimenting with a new pattern for UAV pilot selection. It is based on 32 hours of flying training on light aircraft – single engine land aircraft. This is followed by UAV instruments qualification programme, lasting two months and 35 hours of simulator training.

In case of the US Navy, for Pioneer UAV, a 16 feet wing span UAV, launched from a launcher, only the Mission Commander is a former aviator. Rest of the UAV operators are enlisted with the aviators' background of air mechanics etc.

It is felt that not only should UAV selection and training be separate, but UAVs must have separate qualifying weapon schools. The normal fliers and UAV fliers could have cross flow into each stream. There are enough similarities apart from pure flying like payload operators, weapon system operators, etc. These similarities will only increase in future as UAVs assume larger functions and are crafted and equipped for live combat operations in air to air role. The air to air combat could be to save itself from enemy interceptors or to shoot hostile UAVs / aircraft.

It is also time that the three Services jointly decide on UAVs operations demarcating area of UAV operations, integral to each service. For example, US Army has over 4034 tactical UAVs compared to 42 plus UAVs with US Navy. The USMC has 32 tactical UAVs compared to 158 large UAVs of USAF.[1] The operation of these UAVs over a live battle space would need

[1] Sipri's Military Balance 2010.

coordination, which can be facilitated by proper demarcation of area of operations, mainly by altitude segregation.

UAVs of medium and high endurance travel over vast distances, cutting across civil air corridors. As the persistence of UAVs increases, an inevitable trend – this crisscross across civil air space would become more frequent. So it would not be too late to arrive at an understanding with DGCA / Civil Aviation Authorities, on devising procedures for UAVs operation in and through civil air space.

The multiple sensors on board aircraft and UAVs have thrown up a big dilemma needing urgent attention. Unlike the past, where imagery information either from space or photo reconnaissance aircrafts, followed a long cycle of demand, executed, developed, printed, analysed, processed and supplied the information to the planner, the new proliferating sensors give one, instant information. The sensors and their capabilities will continue to grow following Moore's Law. So, in future, the multitude of sensors will continue to give vast amounts of information, direct to the user. How then one should plan to take out actionable intelligence from this vast information, in real time if possible, is the big question. Where will the intelligence officer be located? Should operations and intelligence merge in to one for best results? Only proper analysis and thereafter trials in operational conditions alone, can provide correct answers because often the sensor itself is a shooter or the shooter has good sensors in its pods. There is no more time for cross checks, extensive fusion with other sources, confirmation from experts and time for decision makers as to what is to be done with real time detected intelligence. So this increasing capability of ISR is making battlefields transparent and poses a very serious question as to how to exploit it optimally.

IAF has never had a dedicated Intelligence branch for air operations. In the past, photo-interpretation was a secondary duty performed by offices trained in this secondary role. This arrangement barely met the needs of peace time intelligence processing. But how can this time consuming model serve the needs of sensor shooter cycle of minutes and seconds? How does the decision maker fit into this sensor – shooter cycle? At what level will the decisions be made? How can we decentralize the decision making? Does the operator also become an Intelligence provider? If so then how should we train for operational and actionable Intelligence?

To add to the complexity of modern war, the sensor – shooter cycle has to be integrated with cyber operations, information operations, electronic warfare etc. and the decision to use lethal weapons or non lethal weapons. If not done properly, then mere possession of modern technology will not suffice to fulfil associated expectations. While some answer will suggest themselves in cerebral inquiry, the real answer will only accrue from operational trials in operational conditions, over and over again. This is inescapable.

9

MODERNISATION OF AIR DEFENCE

With the operation of AFNET (Air Force Network), Indian Air Force has achieved a major milestone in the ongoing modernisation of air defence in India. The five nodes of IACCS (Integrated Air Command and Control Systems) being established, will also ride the AFNET backbone, integrating all ground based and airborne sensors and air defence weapons. The automated IACCS will enable quick transfer of data from low level transportable radars, high power static radars and medium power radars. The AFNET replaces the old communication network set-up using the tropo – scatter technology inducted within the IAF in late 1960S. However, before we examine further requirements of modern air defence system to serve the Indian need in future, it will be relevant to peep into the history of air defence as it evolved on this sub-continent.

The IAF was formed on 01 Apr 1933. However, till attaining independence the only role assigned to IAF was Army cooperation, which entailed visual reconnaissance, message dropping and providing fire support to ground troops. On the eve of World War II, the major roles of air power, including air defence, remained with the RAF in India and the 10th USAAF deployed in India, during World War II. Against the then prevailing Japanese air threat, at its peak the Allies had deployed 64 fighter squadrons of RAF, 28 squadrons of Mitchel B-25 bombers of 10th USAAF and 52 operational radars. There would have been a total of 1632 Allied aircrafts against the Japanese aircraft strength of 740. The nine fighter squadrons of the IAF continued in the role of supporting General Slim's 14th Army. It did not participate in Air defence.

The Japanese ruled the skies as they advanced into South East Asia, moving rapidly towards Myanmar (Burma). In Apr 1942 alone, Japanese air attacks sank about 100 ships in the Bay of Bengal. It would take sustained air action by allies to wrest back the control of air, by the start of 1944. The stark lesson is that but for the control of air, the British would have nearly lost India to the Japanese. Thus, the centrality of air superiority in war.

However, air defence, post independence got little attention. This neglect would haunt our decision makers on the eve of 1962 Sino – Indian War. The imaginary fear of the Chinese Air Force, bombing cities of Kolkata and Delhi, in reprisal to our use of combat air force, prevented us from its use, even though the Chinese had penetrated into our territory. It made us plead with the British and Americans, to provide us with Air defence against further Chinese threats. It led to the first proper air defence exercise with American help, called Ex Shiksha, in 1963, which laid the foundation of initial air defence of India.

From the early days of scattered air defence that looked at only the threatened vital areas facing the west, now air defence has come a long way. India has included a number of medium powered static radars, low level transportable radars, Aerostat radars and AWACS. It is these which have been interconnected on the AFNET. Thus, a large portion of Air space is now under surveillance. But it is not yet complete or fool proof. That is why IAF still wants major inclusion of long range surveillance radars, and high power radars to bolster the air defence. This comes after IAF has already inked contracts for 19 LLTRs (Low Level Transportable Radars), four MPRs (Medium Power Radars) and 30 indigenous medium range Rohini radars.

Plans are also afoot to procure nine more Aerostat radars, to add to the two WL/M 2083 Israeli Aerostats inducted earlier as well as two additional AWACS, to supplement the first three Israeli Phalcon AWACS.[1] As per a report in Aviation Week & Space Technology, the Indian Navy as well as the Indian Army has evinced interest in Lockheed Martin's airships which feature L-88 radar. These could be acquired under transfer of technology protocol.[2]

---

[1] Times of India, 23 Sep 2010

[2] Aviation Week and Space Technology, 12 Jul 2010, p. 33

Radars are used to detect intruders. Thereafter, it is the task of air defence fighters and surface to air missile (SAM) along with anti aircraft artillery (AAA) to shoot down the hostile intruders before they are able to release their bombs and missiles. Air Chief Marshal Pradeep Vasant Naik stated that half of the equipment at his command, faces obsolescence, with that label applying to the majority of air defence weapons.[3] That situation is now being remedied. By Mar 2011, IAF will begin receiving the first of 18 Israeli Aerospace Industries Rafael Spyder quick reaction medium range missile systems. In addition, indigenous Akash SAM induction is likely to commence in Feb 2011. Some more SAM development is ongoing at DRDO, in collaboration with IAI of Israel and with MBDA of France. Thus, it would be another 4 -5 years before IAF has a reasonable number of multi – range SAMs.

The fighter interceptor beef up plans are afoot in the form of the MMRCA project and the fifth generation fighter project is in the pipeline. These additions and plans do present an optimistic picture of air defence modernisation. However, air defence today and increasingly in future will pose many more challenges which demand urgent attention at doctrinal level followed by organisational and operational level.

The air defence threats today include ICBMs, MRBMs, SRBMs, TBMs, SSMs, cruise missile, 'Katyusha' type home grown rockets, and UAVs, in addition to traditional bomber threats of earlier years. For now let us examine more relevant threats in our area. These are aircrafts, cruise missiles, and ballistic missiles starting from 100 km range to around 3000 kms. How can we plan the most optimal defence against these threats?

In the background, we need to keep in mind the most enduring principle of warfare. The best defence is Offence. It is so, for many reasons which we need not go into at this moment. This was the foundation of Cold-War defence since there was no fool proof defence against ICBMs. Offense as first strike or second strike provided the only meaningful defence.

Having ensured a reasonable offense, nations then build certain amount

---

[3] Aviation Week and Space Technology, 11 Oct 2010, p. 30

of defence, including air defence as a prudent choice. All nations follow this - the difference being in the ratio between defence and offence. We must look at air defence with the above, in the background.

Air defence against hostile aircraft is understood well and it is in place. Air defence against UAVs and cruise missile is also not too different. The additional challenge is posed against supersonic cruise missiles and stealthy UAVs. The latter are normally slow speed, at least, will be, till the next decade. Being smaller in cross section, they need to be detected earlier, for which phased array radars and AESA (Active Electronically Scanned Array) radars are more appropriate. One approach for cruise missile defence, as adopted by USA, is the Area Cruise Missile Defence (ACMD) concept by Joint Forces Command. ACMD ties together existing sensors and weapons of Army, Navy and Air Force, including NORAD, to detect cruise missile threat.[4]

This brings us to AFNET. It is understood that AFNET connects sensors and weapons of only IAF. Air defence is indivisible. USSR abused this principle and suffered. Afterwards it corrected this mistake in the Russian Republic. This means that in India too, all air defence weapons and sensors should ideally be networked for centralized control and decentralized execution. These would include Army, Navy, Coast Guard and Air Force.

Next important consideration is proliferation of missiles in Pakistan and China. In fact, one analyst already claims missile gap for India as compared to Pakistan. The implications are clear. A conventionally weak Pakistan will recourse early to missiles, in the next war. Or Jihadi elements, in future could launch a Hezbollah type rocket / missile terror attack against India. What is the best defence against this type of threat?

This is a tough question. Lets us begin at one end of the spectrum and move lower down to find possible solutions. There was no effective defence against ICBMs during Cold War. There is none even today. Defence against shorter range MRBMs and SRBMs is still being fashioned by countries like USA, Japan, and Israel. The expected threat is a few missiles from nations

---

[4] Jane's International Defence Review, Apr 2004, p. 15

like North Korea, Iran etc. Efforts are on to develop missile defence against these, which include boost phase defence, terminal high altitude defence, and mid-course intercepts. These plans do not have high degree of assurance but are one of the solutions in a mixed bag of multiple ways to deal with such threats.

A look at the Israeli system will give us some idea about possible missile defence architecture for India. Israeli missile defence is based on combination of Arrow Weapon System (AWS), co-developed by IAI and Boeing Company. It uses phased array radars called Green Pine. Israel has a National Missile Defence command and control centre to integrate AWS, Patriot missiles and Aegis class ships which house Standard SM-3 missile in missile defence role. Israeli new UAV called Eitan is also integrated for missile defence. One of its tasks is to locate mobile ballistic missile launchers and attack them. Also for boost phase intercept, Israelis were developing another system called Sniper, sensor to shooter system. The AWS comprise Green Pine radar, Citron Tree – fire control centre, Hazel Nut launch centre and operational launchers. AWS is meant as an upper layer defence of Tel Aviv and Haifa cities. Patriot is for defence at lower layer. In addition, successful tests have also been done, using F-15 launching air to air missiles against threatening missiles. The entire system is the responsibility of Israeli Air Force. Needless to state, there is full cooperation between Israelis and Americans, in developing missile defence.

As per DRDO reports India too is developing a missile defence system using Israeli Green Pine Radar and indigenous interceptor missiles. DRDO also claims Akash to be missile defence capable SAM. Sword Fish, Israeli radar is also being integrated. Dr Saraswat of DRDO stated Indian missile to be superior to Russian S-300 PMU and the American Patriot PAC-2. However all this is in developmental stage. What is important to remember is that air defence, a responsibility entrusted to IAF by the government, must remain indivisible and centralized under one agency. One can not separate missile defence from other air threats and have it under two separate agencies. Rather, all the development work, to begin with, must involve the user fully. This helps in proper development. Development in isolation from actual operational conditions, often results in fragmented progress. Lastly one must not forget that air defence is only one of the arrows present in the quiver, to deal with the problem. It is not the sole means.

Next is the threat of short range missiles and rockets. These give little reaction time for defence. Katyusha, a ten feet long rocket having 122 mm diametre and a speed of Mach 3 has a flight time of only 15- 40 seconds. During the 2006 Lebanon conflict, the Israeli Air Force significantly damaged Hezbollah's medium and long range rocket capability, by offensive action. Fajr – 3, Fajr -5, Zeizal – 1, Zeizal – 2, Raad and Khaiber rocket sites were attacked precisely. But it had little success against katyusha rockets. Israel has been developing a short range missile defence interceptor called Stunner. Stunner is based on Rafael Python dual wave imagine infra – red missile technology. Also considered are Oerlikon Contraves Sky shield ground based air defence system; the very rapid fire Metalstorm of Australia and the American Phalanx close in rapid fire system.

The review shows that modernisation of our air defence system is still a way to cope with all the threats. We would need to explore all the avenues of defence in a holistic manner to arrive at the most optimum solution. We also need to start looking at technologies, dealing with foliage penetration, radar, underground radar, and passive radars. In spite of the Purulia arms dropping incident, we are nowhere near integration of civil and military air space, in a proper manner. This too must be done, sooner than later.

10

DOCTRINE & TRAINING

"Our duty is to put ideas into their heads, they will do the rest. This is what is to be done in India"

-Swami Vivekanand

RMAs have occurred throughout the history of warfare. However, most people tend to associate RMA with technology alone. This is only part of the success story. For a true RMA to occur, militaries need to align their technology with doctrine or vice versa. Thereafter, they must put it to vigorous trials and training. In each and every battle fought between the British and Indian States during 18th and 19th century, it was the Indian side which had more and better weapons and larger armies. The success behind British victories were superior generalship combined with rock like discipline of the British Infantry, that is their doctrine and training.

So, trying to reorganise for maximizing new technology will only be the first step. We will need to align our doctrine to technology. If the doctrine is paramount then we will have to be careful in selecting technologies that support the doctrine. As an example, American defence starts in the lands of South Korea, Japan and Europe. Israel's defence lies in its offensive capability. On the eve of World War II, France's doctrine was defensive at the Franco – German border. Our doctrine too will need to suit our requirements at different fronts and spectrums of war. Geographical realities of the huge Himalayan range and likely adversaries will have to be factored.

Having decided doctrinal and technological issues, we will have to tackle other important issues which for want of a better term I call "cultural issues". It is well understood that modern warfare is an extremely complex undertaking. It involves a system of systems, all intricately linked. But linking properly each system itself and thereafter with other systems is the most challenging part for traditionally driven Armies, Air forces and Navies, not to mention, other agencies involved in ISR. This is where the culture comes in.

The basis for integrated warfare is a flexible cultural mind set, willing to first look at the overall bigger picture, before it's own limited picture defined by it's role and part in a war/battle. That this is against natural human inclination is proved by the Gold Water Nichols act of 1986 in USA, which mandated the Services to follow a certain path for integration. Creation of more joint unified commands, culminating in Joint Forces Command in USA, bears testimony. How can one then bring about the cultural change in the stereotypical mind set? The easy answer is to use all possible means. First it needs to be mandated at the highest level. The various reorganisations in the US Military is more the result of law makers than the Services themselves. Reorganisation in Russian military, post Cold War and Chinese military, post – economic reforms was again, mostly, State directed. The next step is proper professional education of the officers, starting as early as possible. Sitting together and studying is less effective for joint-ness, then studying purposely for joint operation even though not co-located. This is where service prejudices seem to cloud the issue on what to study and for how long. One way to approach the issue is to put joint exercises as the primary means of learning rather than year long courses, at various stages. Let practicality be the teacher. What works in the field – that's what we need to study. What fails, needs to be discarded or minimized. Needless to say, the exercises need to be as realistic as possible.

Another cultural change required is in the decision making. The well connected networked system makes way too much information available at many levels. The very senior levels, which normally deal at the strategic level, now have access to too many details. It can be an ongoing action, at a platoon level or a UAV, locking on to a suspected terrorist. This profusion of information creates a decision dilemma for senior leadership in the media sensitive world. What if the suspected terrorist is an innocent civilian – a woman or child in disguise? How to further confirm the identity? Or to let the juniors go on with the mission, hopefully with pre-decided rules of engagement? Well, War is always about blood and gore; death and destruction. While collateral damage has been reduced well out of proportion, compared to the past few decades, it cannot be eliminated totally. The temptation to over control will have to be controlled.

Hence, some statistics from Israel's experience in irregular warfare is educative. Israeli Air Force caries out tasks to prevent infiltrations, to enforce curfews; to liquidate terrorist cells and to destroy illicit weapons caches. It participates in urban anti-terror war. It does all this by innovative application of air power. The following tables point to their effectiveness.

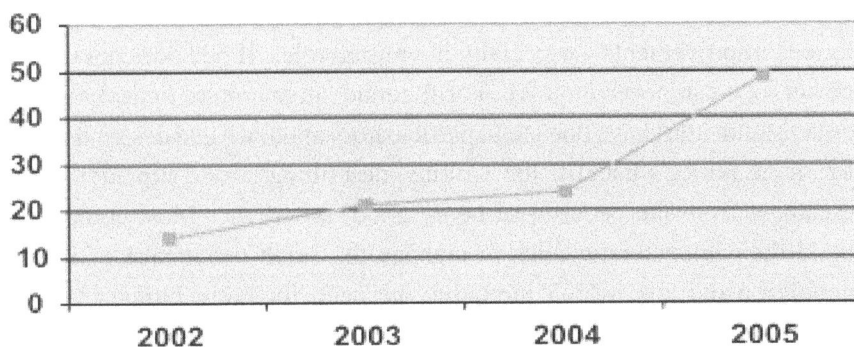

Percentage of Terrorists Killed by Air strikes

Of all the terrorist killed in 2002, Air strikes accounted for only 15%. By 2005 air power was responsible for 50% terrorists killed.[1] Regarding collateral damage, in 2002, one civilian was killed for each militant. By 2005 one civilian was killed for 12 militants killed.

1:1   12 : 1

2002   2005

Collateral Killings. Militants : Civil

---

[1] Defence News, 28 Feb 2005, p.9

The above success resulted from a cumulative effort of intelligence agencies, both civil and military; special command and control cells for decision making; new technology in precision weapons and fusing policy and lastly the complete networked system supported by extensive automation in data mining tools, data structuring tools, cyber space, intelligence processing etc. leading to integrated use of airborne sensors.

Innovations do not happen by themselves. They happen to fulfil various requirements after creative thinking and resort to the untried. The new requirements emerge only when one exercises all available systems and discovers the need for something new or different. Then bright minds, dealing with the exercise come out with innovation. Air Power has to be used first to seek improvements – especially in unusual roles. If one does not use air power, one can never improve. For the innovative culture to develop, the organisation must have openness, participatory approach and design its rules for the majority's benefit. Jim Collins, describing how companies reach greatness from the pedestal of being good, stated, "... Most companies build their bureaucratic rules to manage the small percentage of wrong people on the bus, which increases the need for more bureaucracy to compensate for incompetence and lack of discipline, which then further drives the right people away, and so forth."[2]

A primary task is to create a culture wherein people have tremendous opportunity to be heard and, ultimately, for the truth to be heard. This requires four basic practices:

1. Lead with questions, not answers.

2. Engage in dialogue and debate, not coercion.

3. Conduct autopsies, without blame.

4. Build red flag mechanisms that turn information in to information that cannot be ignored.

---

[2] Jim Collins, "Good to Great – Why some Companies make the Leap and Others don't," Harper Business, New York, 2001. p. 121.

Col. Douglas C. Cato was awarded the Aviation Week & Space Technology's Laureates Award for Maintenance, Repair and Overhaul in 2010. Cato is the commander of the US Air Force's 76th Aircraft Maintenance Group. The award was given to him for processing improvement initiatives in his group that significantly reduced the time and cost of maintenance and servicing of KC-135 aircraft. The group's initiative improved throughout in the inspection docks by 31% and reduced the queue time to four days from twenty six, while generating a savings of $ 1.1 million per aircraft.[3] This was an excellent result of participative approach.

So coming back to our context, we need to relook the following issues. Our prognosis revealed that war on terror and insurgency will occupy our major attention in the coming decades. If this be so, then we need to expand upon the current limited thoughts on air power and counter insurgency. With phenomenal technological advances, immense new possibilities have opened up for utilising air power in counter insurgency roles. We need to try out all these in realistic test like situations. Testing and trials will lead to the best practices and procedures. Doctrinally, we must believe in increasing effectiveness of air power in CI role. Even USA has updated its CI doctrine in 2006 under leadership of Lt Gen David H. Petraeus. Called FM 3-24; MCWP 3-33.5, it runs into 282 pages. The same General then put it in to practice to stabilise Iraq from 2008 onwards and later in Afghanistan in 2010-11. Both places saw positive results.

Our doctrine then should lead to operational directives based on actual tried out procedures in the field. In any case they have been long overdue for updating. The trials will also show us the way for optimum integration for ISR between all involved agencies and better inter-service procedures for use of air power. This will reduce the enormous footprint of deployed personnel on the ground, while at the same time dramatically shrink the freedom envelope of the insurgents. Politically, it would reduce the feeling of alienation of the locals.

---

[3] Aviation Week & Space Technology/ January 10, 2011. p.49.

Our theoretical training, especially for joint warfare has resulted in near absence of new ideas, innovations and ideas to harness emerging technologies. We need to reduce the emphasis on this classroom training. Instead our joint exercises in the field must become the learning ground. What works in the field, then, should become primary learning and basis for theoretical training. Giving full freedom to participants, especially the younger lot will throw up a host of new solutions, for complex operations. More so, in trials involving cyber war, IW and new technologies.

BIBLIOGRAPHY

Books & Publications

Tiwary, A. K., "Air Power & Counter Insurgency" Lancer Books, New Delhi, 2002.

Tiwary, A. K., "Attrition in Air warfare" Lancer Publishers, New Delhi, 2000.

Lambeth, Benjamin S., "Air Power Against Terror - America's Conduct of Operation Enduring Freedom" RAND, 2006.

Lee, David A., "Close Support-Setting Conditions for Success in the Objective Force" Air University, Maxwell Air Base, Alabama, USA, 2003.

Gen Wesely Clark, "Waging Modern Wars" Public Affairs, New York, 2001.

Gen John A. Shaud Ph.D, "USAF Strategy-Past, Present and Future 2018-2023" Air Force Research Institute, Air University, Maxwell Air Base, Alabama, 2009.

Collins, Jim, "Good to Great - Why some Companies make the Leap and Others don't" Harper Business, New York, 2001.

Lt Col James R. Brungees, "Setting the Context - SEAD & Joint War Fighting in uncertain World" Air University, Maxwell Air Base, Alabama, 1994.

Maj Terrance J. Mccaffrey, "What Happened to the BAI? Army & Air Force Battlefield Doctrine Development From Pre Desert Storm to 2001" School of Advanced Air Power Studies, Air University, Alabama, 2002.

Hanlon, Michael O., "Defence Strategy" Brookings Institute, Washington, 2003.

Sqn Ldr Rana T S Chinna, " The Eagle Strikes- The Royal Indian Air Force 1932-1950" Ambi Knowledge Resource Pvt Ltd, New Delhi, 2006.

Reed, Thomas C., "At The Abyss- An Insider's History of the Cold War" Ballintine Books, New York, 2004.

Murray, William, "Strategy For Defeat - The Luftwaffe 1933- 1945" Air University, Alabama, 1983.

Murray, William & Maj Gen Robert H. Scales, Jr, "The Iraq War- A Military History" Natraj Publishers, Dehradun, 2006.

Air Force(USAF) Doctrine Document: "Counter Land Operations" Aug 1999.

"The US Bombing Survey: 30 Sep 1945" Air University Press, Alabama, October 1997.

US Air Force Weapons School, "SSS 600 A: Introduction to Precision Guided Munitions" Nellis AFB, Nevada, Mar 2003.

US Army Field Manual 3-9, "Doctrine For Fire Support-Final Draft" Washington: US Government Printing Office, 2002.

Stephen P. Cohen & Sumit Dasgupta, "Arming without Aiming: Indian Military Modernisation," Version 16-1, 10 Mar 2010.

Magazines/Periodicals

Kislyakov, Andrej, "New Wars and Space Weapons" India Strategic - Jun 2007.

Gp Capt Alistair Byford, "Combined and Joint Lessons" Air Power Review, Summer 2008.

Gp Capt R M Poole, "The Utility of Air Power in Nation Building" RAF Air Power Review, Summer 2005.

Gooderson, Ian, "The British Air-Land Experience in the Second World War" Air Power Review, Autumn 2006.

Lt Gen (Retd) Deve Deptula & Col Mike Francisco, "Air Force ISR Operations" Air & Space Power Journal, 2010 Fall.

Maj Andrew Roe, " Air Power on the North West Frontier of India," Air Power Review, Summer 2008.

Cox, Sebastian, " The Air/Land Relationship-a Historical Perspective 1918-1991" Air Power Review, Summer 2008.

Wing Commander Harv Smith, "From Conningham to Project Connigham Keys" Air Power Review, Spring 2007.

Aviation Week & Space Technology. 4 Sep, 2000, 23 Sep, 2002, 4 Nov, 2002, 11 Nov, 2002, 5 Apr, 2004, 30 May, 2005, 26 Sep, 2005, 27 Mar, 2006, 25 Feb, 2010, 5 Apr, 2010, 31 May, 2010, 7 Jun, 2010, 20 Sep, 2010, 12 Jul, 2010, 11 Oct, 2010, 10 Jan, 2011.

Defence News: 10 Sep, 2001, 18 Aug, 2003, 8 Mar, 2004, 2 Aug, 2004, 28 Feb, 2005, 31 Oct, 2005, 26 Sep, 2006.

Jane's Defence Weekly, "UAV Payload Development" 21 Jul 2004.

Jane's International Defence Review: Sep 1999, Sep 2002, Aug 2003, Apr 2004.

Military Balance, SIPRI-2010

News Week 06 Aug 2007

Newspapers

Times of India: Delhi Edition: 27 Jun, 2007, 8 Jul, 2007, 23 Sep, 2010, 6 Oct, 2010.

Speeches

ACM Sir John Alison, AOC-IN –C Strike Command RAF, speech at RUSI-Trenchard Memorial Lecture, 24 Nov, 1998.

CAS ACM Sir Stephan Dalton-Lecture at Royal Aeronautical Society, 2009.

RAF CAS- speech at Information Security Conference, 2010.

Internet

http://www2.afsoc.af.mil/news/story.asp?id=12328914&http://www.airforcetimes.com/news/2010/10/airforce.air.strike-jtac-1008101.

Lt Col Stout J, "CAS Using Armed UAVs," The Naval Institute Proceedings, Jul 2005, at www.military.com/New Content/113190 N 1-0705-air-p2,—.htm

Index

A

Acoustic Sensors 42

Active Electronically Scanned Array 120

Advance Tactical Missiles 69

Advanced Laser Targeting System 84

Advanced tactical missile 97

Air Component Commander 52

Air Defence Command 10

Air Force Network 117

Air Ground Operations School 83

Air interdiction 68

Air Liaison Officer 74

Air Marshal Sir John Slessor 17

Air Operations Centre 49, 50

Air Superiority 9, 10, 13, 14, 18, 20, 21, 22, 32, 33, 57, 76, 81, 104, 118

Air Tasking Order 52

Air Vice Marshal Conningham 13

Andrei Kislyakov 37

Area Cruise Missile Defence 120

Arrow Weapon System 121

Asymmetric wars 6

AWACS 5, 57, 58, 59, 63, 64, 71, 85, 113, 118

B

Battle field air interdiction 68

Battle of Kasserine Pass 9

Benjamin S. Lambeth 60

Beqqa Valley 3

Blue Flag 58

Bosnia 3

Brahmos Cruise Missiles 95

Brilliant Anti Tank 97

C

CAO 5

CAS 3, 4, 5, 11, 12, 17, 20, 82, 83, 84, 86, 87, 88, 94, 96, 97, 131, 132

Central Air Command 49

Close air support (CAS) 3, 69

Combined Air Operations Centre 51

Command of Air 14

Computer Network Operations 103

Counter insurgency 4

Counter Surface Force Operations 68

Cyber Ops 65

Cyber War 101
  Evolution 102

Cyber Warfare 99

Czech Air Force 21

D

DARPA 45

Department of Homeland Security 104

Desert war in Tunisia 9

Destroy Armor Munitions 97

Distributed Common Ground System 54

Dunkirk 23

E

Eastern Air Command 49

Electronic Systems Centre 58

Electronic Warfare 101

Enhanced Position Location Reporting System (EPLRS) 46

EO Sensors 41

External Pilot 113

F

Fareed Zakaria 24

Fibre optic cables 25

Fire Support Coordination Line 69

Forward Air Controller 82

Full Motion Video 43, 56

G

Gen Wesley K. Clark 39

General Karl Eikenbery 35

General Sir Auchinleck 13

Global information Grid 54

Gold Water Nichols Act 124

Gotha Bombers 12

Ground Laser Target Designator 84

Gulf War Air power Survey 71

H

Hyper Spectral Sensors 41

I

Imaging IR Sensors 41

Infrared Zoom Laser Illuminator Designator 46

Integrated Air Command and Control Systems 117

Integrated Target System 84

Internal Pilot 113

IR Sensors 41

J

Joint Direct Attack Munitions 92

Joint Force Air Component Commander 52

Joint Forces Command 120

Joint Standoff Weapon 92

Joint Task Force 104

Joint Terminal Attack Controller 82

Joint Unmanned combat air systems 45

K

Kargil operations 34

Kill Boxes 75

Korean War 10

L

Lord Gort 23

Lord Trenchard 16

Low Level Transportable Radars 118

Luftwaffe 13, 18, 19, 20, 21, 22, 23, 51, 66, 88, 130

M

Maginot Line 18

Malacca straits 4

Master Air Attack Plan 52

Medium Power Radars 118

Modern Battlefield 37

MTI Radar 42

Multi Spectral 41

Multiple Rocket Launchers 94

N

Nani A. Palkhiwala 1

O

Operations Cobra 10

P

P 47 Thunderbolt 9

P-51 Mustang 9

Predator B 46, 47, 79, 95

Prithvi II 95

R

Radars 42

Receive Only Video Enhanced Receiver 56

Receive only Video Enhanced Receiver (ROVER) 43

S

Samuel P. Huntington 24

Sea Power 2

SEAL 90

Sensor Fused Weapons 94

Small Diametre Bomb 93

South Western Air Command 49

Southern Air Command 49

Space Command 104

Space Control Cell 63

Special Operation Forces 77

Stephan P. Cohen 52

Strategic Air Command 10

Strategic Bombing 9

Suez Canal 4

Synthetic Aperture Radar 42

T

Tactical Air Command 10

Tactical Air Control Centre 72

Tactical Air Control Party 84

Tactical Control Party 88

Tactical Targeting Network Technology 59

Terminal Attack Controller 82, 83

Theatre Missile Defence 59

Thomas Friedman 38

Total War 2

Transparency of the Battlefield 40

Trusted thin Client 59

U

UAVs 5, 6, 26, 41, 43, 44, 45, 46, 47, 48, 51, 55, 56, 76, 87, 88, 90, 96, 113, 114, 115, 119, 120, 132

Global Hawk 47

Hermes 50 47

Heron 47

Predator B 47

Ultra Spectral 41

W

Western Air Command 49

Wide Area Search Autonomous
    Attack Miniature Munit 93

Wind Corrected Munitions Dispens-
    ers 92

Wolfram Von Richthofen 19

Z

Zeppelin air ships 12

www.ingramcontent.com/pod-product-compliance
Lightning Source LLC
Chambersburg PA
CBHW060421100426
42812CB00030B/3261/J